M000206837

This book restores to business thinking much of the common sense and time-polished wisdom that modern economic thinking has leached away.

Rory Sutherland, Vice Chairman, Ogilvy UK

As business leaders we have an innate feeling that we have to have our team follow us and through them we achieve extraordinary results together. Unfortunately our business training and education all tend to focus on the tangible – results, KPIs, budgets and measurements, and through time these turn the focus upside down and our people somehow become means to an end rather than ends themselves and we become trapped in inhumane work environments over and over again. This book offers a real path to change for frustrated leaders and is a must-read for those who have the courage to take the first step towards making their work environment humane again – fertile ground for them and their team to flourish and contribute greatly to customers, the organization and themselves.

Savio Kwan, former President and COO, Alibaba

At a time when trust in leadership – in business, government and civil society – is fast eroding, this book is timely, asking you powerful questions about your own meaning and purpose as a leader. The most profound answers lie in values and philosophy, which have been neglected in the world of leadership education until now. The four authors rightly place these centre stage.

Dame Julie Mellor, Chair, Demos and The Young Foundation; former Chair, Equal Opportunities Commission and Parliamentary and Health Service Ombudsman

How can I flourish in an organization while helping colleagues and the organization itself to flourish? This great challenge of the modern world demands a personal response. The authors of this inspiring book evoke philosophers ancient and contemporary, bringing their insights to life as guides to wise and humane leadership.

Professor John Y Campbell, Economics Department, Harvard University

This book challenges the way we think about leadership, the habits and conventions that have become so ingrained that we are no longer aware of them. We are used to changing our processes, structures and systems with mixed results. It is time to take a long look in the mirror and ask ourselves deep questions about what it means to be a leader, a leader who wants to flourish and wants others to flourish. These are questions of philosophy.

Professor Nandu Nandkishore, Indian School of Business; former Global Executive Board Member, Nestlé SA, Switzerland

A good manager is always recognized for their curiosity and ability to question themself. To develop these skills, philosophy is certainly one of the best fields of exploration that exists.

Franck Mougin, Director of Human Resources, Vinci

This book is for leaders who may want to refresh their leadership practice. It puts you on the spot, bringing a series of philosophers into your life who will raise questions about you and your purpose that cannot be ducked. Leadership is a lifelong journey, and who better as travel companions than quarrelsome Marx and impish Isiah Berlin? Socrates, Popper, the Buddha and so many others have been wonderfully reinterpreted for our modern, uncertain and turbulent world. This book is a double gift of leadership wisdom and philosophical teachings – it's readable, funny and very very wise!

Shaks Ghosh CBE, Chief Executive, Clore Social Leadership Foundation

This book is a unique and powerful blend of the insights of philosophers and the authors' extensive practical experience of change management. Reading it will challenge every leader to look again at what empowerment means, how organizations really function, and why human values of fairness and trust are vital for sustainable success in the modern economy.

Sir Martin Donnelly, President, Boeing Europe; former Permanent Secretary, UK Department of International Trade

Organizations are obsessed with 'Doing' and 'Knowing' and do not create time and space for 'Being'. This book is provoking us to start a new conversation that will bring more meaning and serve the well-being of all.

Anil Sachdev, Founder and CEO, School of Inspired Leadership, Gurgaon, India

To be a successful leader of a modern, sustainable, purpose-led organization that recognizes its responsibilities to the communities it serves, needs more than skills and ability – it needs authenticity. Authenticity is based in a deep leadership philosophy that inspires the individuals leaders seek to lead to take personal responsibility to do the right thing in every interaction they have with others. People want to be empowered, respected and fulfilled at a human level in today's workplace and to know that the values of the organization they work for not only match their own values but are embodied and evidenced consistently in the leaders they work with. *What Philosophy Can Teach You About Being a Better Leader* gives those who have been given the privilege of leadership new thinking and practical learning to successfully fulfil their roles by recognizing the need for those they seek to inspire to be engaged with meaning and purpose.

Sir Ian Powell, Chair, Capita plc

In a world dominated by AI, algorithms, bots and big data, great leadership is about being a good human. And philosophy provides powerful insights into what that means.

Professor Chris Styles, Dean, UNSW Business School, Sydney, Australia

An engaging, persuasive and radical study of what it means to live the good life at work. The authors guide the reader through a fascinating philosophical landscape, posing a decisive challenge to

conventional leadership thinking, and offering a new and humane model in terms of which to comprehend one's role in the workplace.
Dr Fiona Ellis, Professor of Philosophy, University of Roehampton

A highly unusual book whose time has come. Four distinguished business school professionals bring long experience and exhilarating fresh thinking to the concept and practice of leadership. And in doing so they break the mould – for it is philosophy, not psychology, that drives this riveting approach. A book that travels from the Buddha and Aristotle via Hobbes, Kant, Nietzsche and many others to Karl Popper and the present day might be dizzying, but the authors ensure that the lessons of philosophy are always relevant and that they are intensely practical. Both relevant and revelatory, this is a real tour de force.
Lord Lisvane (Sir Robert Rogers), former Clerk and Chief Executive, House of Commons

Well-researched and clearly written, this book reminds us of the human being at the centre of business. Business is not all about data, efficiency and output, but overcoming isolation and allowing human beings to flourish. This is an important message in a world becoming ever more governed by technology.
Robert Roland Smith, philosopher, and author of *Breakfast with Socrates*

What Philosophy Can Teach You About Being a Better Leader

Alison Reynolds

Dominic Houlder

Jules Goddard

David Lewis

KoganPage

First published in Great Britain and the United States in 2020 by Kogan Page Limited

2nd Floor, 45 Gee Street	122 W 27th St, 10th Floor	4737/23 Ansari Road
London	New York, NY 10001	Daryaganj
EC1V 3RS	USA	New Delhi 110002
United Kingdom		India

www.koganpage.com

© Alison Reynolds, Dominic Houlder, Jules Goddard and David Lewis, 2020

ISBNs
Hardback   978 1 78966 026 5
Paperback   978 0 7494 9316 5
eBook   978 0 7494 9317 2

British Library Cataloguing-in-Publication Data

A CIP record for this book is available from the British Library.

Library of Congress Cataloging-in-Publication Data

Names: Reynolds, Alison (Business consultant), author.
Title: What philosophy can teach you about being a better leader / Alison
  Reynolds, Dominic Houlder, Jules Goddard, David Lewis.
Description: London ; New York, NY : Kogan Page, 2020. | Includes
  bibliographical references and index. |
Identifiers: LCCN 2019036568 (print) | LCCN 2019036569 (ebook) | ISBN
  9781789660265 (hardback) | ISBN 9780749493165 (paperback) | ISBN
  9780749493172 (ebook)
Subjects: LCSH: Leadership. | Philosophy.
Classification: LCC HD57.7 .R4935 2020 (print) | LCC HD57.7 (ebook) | DDC
  658.4/092–dc23

Typeset by Integra Software Services, Pondicherry
Print production managed by Jellyfish
Printed and bound by CPI Group (UK) Ltd, Croydon CR0 4YY

CONTENTS

About the authors xiii
Preface xv
Acknowledgements xvii

Introduction: The dehumanized workplace 1

Why philosophy matters 1
How we lost our humanity at work 3
Alienation is the curse of both leaders and led 5
How this book will work 8
Note 14

01 Who can reconnect us with our dreams? 15

Your dream job and funeral eulogy 15
Psychologists' advice about the good life 16
What's wrong with feeling good? 18
Doing what's good for you 20
Summary 22
Questions 22
Notes 23

02 Reason and passion in the humanized workplace 25

Who was Aristotle? 25
Aristotle's middle way 26
A workplace for slaves? 27
A workplace for animals? 28
Nietzsche takes us beyond reason 30
The end of moral authority 32
Breaking away from the herd 33
Life as a work of art 34
The Nietzschean workplace 35

Summary 38
Questions 39
Notes 39

03   Humanizing strategy 41

The rise of the strategist 41
Strategy and inhumanity 43
Is your strategy about capturing value from others – or
    creating it? 45
The Buddha's strategy advice 48
A philosophy of connectedness in action 50
From goal to path 54
Summary 56
Questions 56
Notes 57

04   Creativity and critical thinking 59

Learning from capital markets 60
Peter Lynch and asymmetric knowledge 62
Warren Buffett and market inefficiency 64
Comparisons and contrasts between Lynch and Buffett 65
Category mistakes in business 66
George Soros and human fallibility 67
Lessons of success from the capital markets 70
Popper's logic of scientific discovery 71
A Popperian theory of corporate strategy, condensed into four
    maxims 72
The paradox of good intentions 75
An open mind 78
Conclusion 79
Questions 80
Notes 80

05   A question of example and fairness 83

A world divided 84
Max Perutz and the Cavendish Laboratory 84
Leading in a spirit of fairness 86

Plutarch's exemplum 88
Organizational behaviour and procedural fairness 90
Fairness in practice 92
A dangerous collusion 97
Questions 98
Notes 99

06   **The gift of authority** 101

Introduction 101
Tell them we feel un-empowered! 101
Problem sorted? 102
What can philosophy tell us about how to use our authority
    to support empowered people? 103
The best of intentions 103
We get it upside down 104
Authority is a gift 106
A question of philosophy 109
Thomas Hobbes – we are born equal 110
Immanuel Kant – we are duty bound 113
The categorical imperative and leadership 115
The chief ethical officer (CEO) 118
Key ideas 120
Conclusion 121
Notes 122

07   **Meaning and communication** 123

The great cascade 124
Why is telling so compelling? 125
The tyranny of the tangible and the fallacy of control 126
Mistaken resistance 127
How we got here – the rise of the omnipotent leader 128
What philosophy tells us 131
The stoic philosophy 131
Understanding how we come to understand 134
Understanding as a social process 135
The road to meaning 136

Commitment to act 138
Three lessons from David Hume 139
A new way – sense making not sense giving 139
Creating a space where anything is possible 140
Summary 141
Questions 141
Notes 142

08   **From engagement to encounter** 143

The annual engagement survey 143
So why this approach? 145
The focus on engagement 146
Is your agenda worthy? 146
The trouble with 'buy-in' 148
Engagement is not the problem 149
What does philosophy tell us? 150
An alternative – encounter 151
How can we embrace encounter? 153
Implications for leadership 156
The real work 158
Changing our practices 159
Being present – a necessity for encounter 161
Summary 163
Questions 163
Notes 164

09   **Values and ethical pluralism** 165

A plethora of values 166
What is the problem to which a value statement
    is the solution? 168
Making it personal 169
In defence of values statements 170
Choosing values as though from a menu 171
The source of moral complexity 173
Objective pluralism 175

Pluralism in practice 176
Moral dilemmas and the middle way 178
Addressing dilemmas 179
The method of reconciliation 181
Conclusions 183
Questions 184
Notes 184

10 **The freedom to do what you can** 187

Be careful what you wish for 188
What can philosophers teach us about our freedom
    to act and our responsibility as leaders? 189
The incident of the cat and the wheelie bin 190
Even if organizations were prisons 191
Socrates – by force of spiritedness 192
No more sweeteners 194
The empowered organization 195
Summary 201
Questions 202
Notes 202

Index 203

ABOUT THE AUTHORS

Alison Reynolds

BSc (York), MSc Sustainability and Responsibility (Ashridge), MA Research in Philosophy (pending, Buckingham)

Alison is a faculty member at Ashridge Executive Education, Hult International Business School where she designs and delivers award-winning executive programmes. In 2019, Alison's name was announced on the Thinkers50 Radar alongside that of David Lewis, in recognition of their work on cognitive diversity. Alison's research and thinking features consistently in the *Harvard Business Review* and she co-developed the Qi Index, a tool used by organizations worldwide to better understand the quality of their interaction. Alison lives in London with her partner and her daughter, Imogen.

Dominic Houlder

MA (Cambridge), MBA (Stanford), MA Research in Philosophy (Buckingham)

Dominic has been a faculty member at London Business School for more than 25 years, where he is a repeated winner of best teacher awards. Previously he worked for the Boston Consulting Group and held senior leadership positions in the corporate world. Dominic oversees his family's business interests in Latin America, while in the non-profit arena he is a Governor of the RNLI and is on the boards of the Clore Social Leadership Foundation and the Karuna Trust. His home is in Scotland, where – alongside his academic and client commitments – he is a crofter on the Isle of Skye. He has been a committed Buddhist practitioner for more than 30 years. He is the co-author of *Mindfulness and Money* (Broadway).

www.dominichoulder.com

Dr Jules Goddard

MA (Oxford), MBA (Pennsylvania), PhD (London), MA Research in Philosophy (Buckingham)

Jules was the first doctoral student at London Business School in 1970. He joined the faculty in 1978 as a Lecturer in Marketing. He edited both the *International Journal of Advertising* and the *London Business School Quarterly*. Since 2000, he has been running a series of action learning workshops for senior executives that he calls 'Discovery Programmes', located in foreign cities, based on creative encounters with extraordinary people and designed to stimulate corporate innovation. Based on these experiences, he has recently co-written, with Tony Eccles, *Uncommon Sense, Common Nonsense* (Profile Books).

www.schoolofuncommonsense.com

David Lewis

BSc (Portsmouth), MSc (Brunel), Thinkers50 Radar 2019

David was appointed Head of Computer Science at London Metropolitan University at the age of 28. His collaboration with the Psychology department gave rise to a pioneering degree focused on people-centred computing systems. Head hunted to join KPMG, David co-founded their change management practice. After five years consulting with international clients, David left KPMG to create a new consulting company that grew rapidly and was successively sold five years later. David stayed in the new venture to run the UK business for three years, before leaving to become an independent consultant and entrepreneur.

David joined London Business School in 2011 as a programme director. He has worked with a number of the school's key clients and on its flagship programme. He brings a unique experiential perspective to helping leaders change their approach to enable others to flourish and innovate.

PREFACE

Our desire to write this book has grown out of the stress and sense of isolation we observe in the leaders we work with across the world. At the same time we hear their desire to create and be part of organizations where people, ideas and performance can flourish.

For all of us, the community within which we work shapes our identity, purpose and sense of belonging. We should strive to create a more human workplace not only for the sake of ourselves but also for the ambitions and hopes of others. Making the world a better place, whether it be in the form of products, services, policy or aid depends on fertile ground in which ideas can be nurtured and everyone's contribution counts and is valued. This is the leadership challenge.

If we look back over recent history we see two perspectives that have informed our ideas about leadership the most – economics, focused on productivity, and psychology, focused on motivation. This book brings in a third perspective – philosophy, asking the questions 'What is good?' 'What is the right thing to do?' Peter Drucker famously said, 'Management is doing things right, leadership is doing the right things.'[1] Deciding what is right is a question of philosophy. Applying philosophy to the challenge of leadership in today's world enables us to explore what the right things are.

It is the human condition to seek meaning. What should we live for? When are we at our most human? What is the 'good life'? The life that we would most like to live has been a major preoccupation for philosophers. We see the good life not in a hedonic sense but in pursuit of articulating what matters most, so that we can flourish. Philosophy is about human flourishing. In this book we apply philosophy to the question of what it means to live the good life at work. We challenge our readers to think differently about their role as leaders, to question conventional leadership thinking, to ask new questions, to change priorities and transform leadership practices.

With the help of great philosophers we will put people and what it means to flourish at the heart of leadership to create organizations in which people, ideas and performance thrive.

(Some of the content in Chapter 5 has been published in the *London Business School Review*.[2])

Notes

1 Drucker, P (2000) *The Essential Drucker: The best of sixty years of Peter Drucker's essential writings on management*, Taylor and Francis
2 Goddard, J (2018) The Power Paradox, *London Business School Review*, **29** (2), May, pp 14–17

ACKNOWLEDGEMENTS

The ideas and ideals that we express in this book are the culmination of many years of conversations with executives on a wide variety of leadership development programmes, delivered mainly at London Business School and Hult Ashridge.

We feel privileged to have worked in settings where so many leaders and managers felt free to express their candid views on the joys, but also the tribulations of today's workplace.

Over the last 30 years or so, we have, between us, designed, directed and delivered leadership development programmes for about 25,000 students and executives from over 200 companies and professional service firms.

For example, we have run strategy workshops for the executive boards of Rolls-Royce, ICL, Orange, Smith System Engineering, the UK Ministry of Defence and Ogilvy. We have led discovery expeditions for senior executives in Prudential, Danone, Ipsen, Liva Nova, Engie and KPMG. We have directed and delivered custom programmes for Oracle, Emirates, GEA, DP World, BUPA, Mars, Freshfields, PwC, SAP, Nestlé, Clariant, Generali, Standard Chartered, Elbit Systems, Menzies, Capita, E&Y, BCR, Ingersoll Rand and Saatchi & Saatchi. And we have worked with many generations of MBA students and Sloan Fellows.

To all the participants on these programmes who, by sharing their experiences of leading – and being led – have been instrumental in shaping our ideas, we owe a debt of gratitude for their generosity of spirit and honesty of expression.

And to our academic and professional colleagues and influencers, who have been particularly supportive of a philosophical approach to business, we are most appreciative: Julie Brennan, John Campbell, Michael Chaskalson, Stephen Coates, Sir Martin Donnelly, Yves Doz, François Dupuy, Fiona Ellis, Tammy Erickson, Giles Ford, Shaks Ghosh, Sumantra Ghoshal, Lynda Gratton, Charles Handy,

Gay Haskins, Peter Hinssen, Samuel Hughes, Richard Jolly, Judie Lannon, Muriel Larvaron, Lance Lee, Sir Andrew Likierman, Costas Markides, Dame Mary Marsh, Lindsey Masson, Jens Meyer, Nandu Nandkishore, Nigel Nicholson, Kathleen O'Connor, François Ortalo-Magné, Rick Price, Chris Rawlinson, Michael Ray, Megan Reitz, Claire-Marie Robilliard, Bob Sadler, Robert Roland Smith, Sir Martin Sorrell, Donald Sull, Rory Sutherland, Doug Tremellen, Debbie Wayth, Bill Weitzel and Ralph Weir.

To Sir Roger Scruton,
Tutor to all four of us,
With affection and admiration

Introduction: The dehumanized workplace

Why philosophy matters

Have you ever felt like a tool in the workplace, a cog in someone else's machine? Might those working for you have ever felt the same?

If so, this book is for you. It is born from our work with leaders and led at every level, from huge global organizations to smaller local ventures, in both public and private sectors and on every continent (except for Antarctica). Again and again we find that those whose lives we touch want to be more fulfilled – more human – in their work, and to help others to be so too.

As authors, we all work in leading business schools, which have the commendable goal of transforming the world of work for the better. What does 'better' mean? For decades, business schools have placed finance and economics centre stage; those disciplines tell us that the better workplace is one that uses resources – including you – more efficiently so that all of us can prosper. Latterly, management psychology has come to the fore. Psychologists go beyond economics to tell us that efficiency and wealth are not enough; the better workplace is one in which we are more emotionally engaged, attuned and feel more positive about our work.

It would be folly to dismiss the importance of wealth creation and employee engagement. Our colleagues in economics and psychology have much to teach us. But there is a missing voice. As well as learning from economists – who show us how to deliver the goods – and from psychologists – who tell us how to feel good – we need to hear from philosophers. Beyond material goods or feeling good, what is good for us? That is the central question that moral philosophy seeks to address. What is good for us is what enables our development and flourishing as human beings.

> In this book we bring to life the voices of great philosophers and hear what they have to say about human flourishing. If you can bring their insights into the workplace – as leader or led – then you and those in your care will no longer be tools or cogs in someone else's machine.

You will be flourishing in a workplace that you have helped to humanize. We will introduce philosophers who explore what it means to be fully human – in contrast to being like an animal with no insight into the good life, or a slave who has no power over herself or the world. During the working week there are many pressures that cause us to act like – or treat others as – slaves or animals. These will not go away, but we can nonetheless find or create many opportunities to behave more like human beings, which is the invitation of this book.

We begin by asking you to reflect on the insights of Karl Marx. This may look like a strange choice for authors coming from the world of business education. None of us can recall Marx ever appearing on the syllabus of any business course, other than fleetingly, to be dismissed as a madman or a monster. But his understanding of our dehumanized condition in the workplace lies at the heart of our concerns. Back in 1844, Marx – then a brilliant young journalist – lamented the plight of industrial workers. These, he said, '... do not fulfil themselves in their work but deny themselves, have a feeling of misery rather than well-being, do not develop freely their mental and physical energies but are physically exhausted and mentally debased. Workers, therefore, feel themselves at home only during their leisure time, whereas at work they feel homeless.'[1]

How we lost our humanity at work

Marx was writing about alienation. This was the price of the extraordinary gains in economic efficiency that were being made across Europe while he wrote. As Marx saw it, the call to efficiency and greater wealth took independent craft workers from their cottages into the industrial mills that were springing up around him. In his romantic view, the craft worker of old had enjoyed autonomy, the pride of creating a finished product rather than just an insignificant piece of it, the sense of control over his or her environment, and the freedom to connect with others. In his ideal world, Marx said, 'Our product would be like so many mirrors in which we saw reflected our essential natures'.

To get efficient, our forebears had to subject themselves to managers who coordinated their individual tasks. Making good use of costly industrial equipment required workplace discipline; workers could not set their own schedules or do as they please. And so, once in the mill, the whistle would define the working day, and the finished product would disappear into a series of finely engineered repetitive process steps with tight orchestration down to individual hand movements. The promised gain would be a higher wage than the independent craft worker could ever earn, but the other side of the bargain would be giving up humanity in a dehumanized work environment. For Marx, this was a Faustian bargain, Faust being the legendary figure in morality tales who sold his soul to the devil in return for material rewards.

Marx saw the impact of industrial conditions at first hand through his long relationship with Friedrich Engels, his friend, generous sponsor and son of a wealthy Lancashire mill owner. He undoubtedly exaggerated the proud independence of the craft worker in the cottage, which might well have been cramped, unsafe and filthy. Commission agents providing raw material and collecting piecework could set harsh terms requiring any small children in the family to take their turn at the loom alongside their parents. But for Marx, workplace alienation was even worse because it denies who we are, making us into human resources rather than allowing us to live as fully fledged human beings.

As an early management guru – Frederick Winslow Taylor – wrote 70 years after Marx's denunciation of workplace alienation, 'In the past the man has been first; in the future the system must be first.'

Marx has long been out of fashion. Marxist economists were discredited intellectually in the 1930s and 1940s, and at the same time the social and political miseries and economic impoverishment of coercive Marxist regimes were coming to the fore. Those systems crashed in the old Soviet Union and Eastern Europe in 1989 and formerly socialist movements disavowed their heritage. Ironically, the only government in the world which today retains Karl Marx in its political sloganeering is China, arguably the world's most successful capitalist project, or as Chinese elites prefer to describe it, 'socialism with Chinese characteristics'. Meanwhile, under government oversight, through the rise of trade unions and the communitarianism that emerged from the 20th century's wars, workplaces became less harsh – offering greater job security, a touch of paternalism and rising wages that kept the sense of alienation at bay.

But now, after the bicentenary of his birth, Marx is back. Most obviously, he has once again become the intellectual backbone of resurgent left-leaning political and social movements across Europe. As just one example, Thomas Picketty's neo-Marxist *Capital in the Twenty-First Century* has outsold every other book on economics since its publication in 2014. Why? Because the revolutions in globalization and technology have made workplaces less human alongside increasing inequality and monopoly power. In the United States, Google and Facebook between them control two-thirds of online advertising, and Amazon, 40 per cent of online shopping. In parts of the world, more than 90 per cent of web searches run through Google. These are the winners. At the other end of the spectrum, most businesses face a tougher and tougher competitive squeeze. They are the organizations in which most of us work.

Here we find the relentless quest for more and more efficiency gains. And it is we who bear the brunt of it. Many of us are finding that our pay fails to keep pace with inflation, that we have less job security as both leaders and led, and ever tighter control of our working lives whether we remain – technically – employees or join the growing army of zero-hours contractors who have no security. While most people reading this book remain rich by historical standards, the old Faustian bargain of greater efficiency for ever greater wealth – except for a few – is over. That bargain held the sense of alienation at bay. But alienation has returned, in full force. Marx's voice from long ago carries vitally important warnings about our workplaces. Even if we set aside Marx's economic and political prescriptions as madness, we would be wise to keep before us his diagnosis of the alienated human condition.

Marx's denunciation of alienation in the workplace is echoed by the many voices that we hear today.

Alienation is the curse of both leaders and led

Take Dolores, a human resources manager for a global French engineering company, based in Bogota. 'We used to have so much freedom', Dolores told us. 'Manfred – that's my old boss – ran the Colombian operation as if it was his own business. Correction – he insisted that all of us on his team saw it as our business. So we did. We gave it body and soul, so many late evenings and weekends, so much fun and togetherness as well. And as Colombians we were proud to be making a real difference to our country with the business we had built up over all those years.'

We asked Dolores why it had all changed, if it was all so great. 'Well', she said, 'it wasn't hugely efficient. The head office team in Lyons was starting to ask us more and more about our cost ratios. We thought that customer care and loyalty – and the premium prices we could charge – more than made up for that, so when the end came it took us all by surprise.' She was referring to the company's massive global restructuring, which had involved one of us authors. 'All the local functions got centralized. They got rid of all the country managers. Manfred became head of Latin American sales. I never see him these days. Two of our Colombian factories got shut down. My last task was to explain why it made sense to source from Argentina. Honestly, words failed me in front of the factory team. All I could say was that it was Group Policy.' She went on to tell us that following the reorganization she was now part of a global function overseeing employee benefits, working mostly from home after the downtown Bogota office closed. 'It's a year since I saw my new boss in Lyons,' she went on to tell us. 'We have endless Skype meetings of course, but with all of his 54 direct reports online I just switch off the video and write my reports. Those reports! My former colleagues think I'm some head office spy.'

The plight of middle managers at the mercy of corporate reorganizations is well known. But how about our MBA students? As educators working in top-ranked business schools, each year we see extraordinarily bright, energetic young people looking to harness their learning to launch stellar careers, in which they will be the masters and mistresses of their universe rather than its victims. For decades, a prize job on graduation from our institutions has been a position with a strategy consulting firm such as Bain, McKinsey or The Boston Consulting Group. Typically, those positions offer the best pay and sometimes generous joining bonuses. But our students don't gravitate to those firms just for the money. There has been the promise of working in small teams of outstanding peers on a varied range of the most demanding challenges faced by the leaders of world-class organizations – and all at the age of 29. But a former student dolefully reported that for all the promise of a life grandly strategizing, the reality was spending over a year analysing one element of the process optimization plan for a small piece of the Saudi Arabian state pension management system.

Those at the top of professional service firms, be they strategy consulting houses, the law, medicine or architecture, do continue to have a high degree of autonomy with pride in their work and identity as trusted advisers to important clients. But even so, as Barbara, a senior partner in a leading global firm put it to us ruefully, her intimate relationship with client CEOs and her own ideas are not the drivers of career success anymore so much as selling vast global processes that no individual professional can own.

'I feel like a cog in the machine,' Barbara told us. She seemed surprised when we pointed out that – as one of the most senior people in her organization – it was her machine.

It became clear that for all Barbara's position of power and substantial partnerial compensation, her trouble – like Dolores and our MBA student – was the sense of being commoditized, no longer having an authentic personal contribution to make, just being a resource, albeit a very high-priced one. She went on to consider the impact of artificial intelligence and robotics in the professional workplace. 'How,' she asked, 'will we ever find the opportunities to train our new young people to become professionals if the entry-level work is all to be mechanized? Will we even need professionals anymore?'

As we researched the challenge of alienation, we found IT workers compelled to codify and part with their expertise, university lecturers bound to deliver standard off-the-shelf courses (with ready-made jokes), countless disengaged middle managers: all alienated from their product, their peers and their identity as human beings in the workplace. What is your experience? You may be working as an employee, or, as time goes on, more likely as a contractor without employment rights in the 'gig economy'. Do you have stories like these, in which you find you are treated – or are treating others – as depersonalized commodities? And if stories like these don't immediately leap to mind, just think about how we relate to time in the current environment. A colleague speaks of 'hurry sickness' as a telltale sign that the pursuit of efficiency is creating an alienated mindset, with no time for our own or others' humanity. Do you, he asks, look for a 30-second task while micro-waving? Get a buzz from just catching a plane or train? Have to do something else when you drive? Eat at your desk (whilst also checking your emails)? Do something else whilst brushing your teeth? Get impatient when waiting in line or in traffic? Find your mobile phone painfully slow? Hate the time it takes to boot up your computer? Want to interrupt other people frequently? Do you do something else in telephone conferences? And – our favourite – do you push the door close button in lifts repeatedly (check this last one in your own office building)? All of these are signs of alienation, that we have lost our minds.

If our stories and observations resonate with you, then this is your book. Our project picks up Karl Marx's challenge. Instead of treating others as commoditized resources and becoming those resources ourselves, we explore what it will take to enable human flourishing in the workplace. We are writing for both the leader and the led. When we speak of leaders, we mean leaders at any level in an organization; indeed, anyone, whether in employment or working as a contractor, who influences how the workplace functions, for good or ill. We speak of the led because those of us following leaders also have a responsibility for our own commoditization – or for our flourishing. Remember, alienation took place around a Faustian pact. Dehumanization was the price we paid for the extraordinary efficiency gains that allowed us to enjoy unparalleled material wealth. Can we now change the terms of the bargain, and enjoy the further enormous gains in efficiency that lie ahead of us with the new technology revolution of AI and robotics, while at the same time recovering our workplace humanity? In this book our answer is yes – provided that as the led we share the responsibility rather than just look to leaders for salvation, and that as leaders we use our power and influence to loosen the chains of alienation.

How this book will work

We owe this book to our students and our clients. We address questions that they have raised and which any of us might ask of our increasingly inhuman, alienated workplaces.

Following this introduction, in Chapter 1 we look at the answers that psychology offers about how to feel less alienated and more engaged. We find that these answers are not enough. The good life – in or out of the workplace – is not for us about feeling good so much as pursuing what is good for us, allowing us to flourish, reaching our fullest potential. Here we see that the answers need to come from the discipline of philosophy, which gives more objective views on the good life. These are ethical views in the old sense of the word 'ethics', derived from the ancient Greek word ethos, which best translates as 'character'. The best life is the one which allows us to most fully develop our human character, through objective philosophical guidance.

In Chapter 2, we introduce our first sources of philosophical wisdom. We ask what two authorities – Aristotle and Nietzsche, who take very different approaches – would make of our contemporary workplaces, and what advice they would give on how to flourish within them, overcoming alienation. Aristotle argued that reason is the distinctive capacity which sets flourishing human beings apart from slaves or animals. Animals are driven by instinct; slaves follow orders. A flourishing person, by contrast, makes her own choices through her own judgements, weighing up her own interests while considering her responsibilities to the community. If Aristotle were to step into a time machine and travel the better part of 2,500 years to the present day, he would be sadly surprised to encounter a lot of semi-disguised slavery in contemporary organizations, as well as an excess of animal spirits. Seen through Aristotle's gaze, leaders have a crucial educational role, helping others to advance their skills in making free, rational choices that will improve their lives. Friedrich Nietzsche, writing in the late 19th century, shared with Aristotle the concern for human flourishing and autonomy, but with a different end in mind. For Nietzsche, to flourish is to excel, to live your life as a work of art. Rather than repressing those animal spirits, Nietzsche invites us to harness the passions for the sake of creativity. Leaders should set their creative workers free and remove any obstacles to their remarkable work. We believe that we need both Aristotelian reason and Nietzschean passion in our organizations and that the leadership task is to enable both, however contradictory that might seem.

Chapter 3 is about strategy: how the direction of our organizations gets defined and implemented. The core assumptions of contemporary strategy unfortunately disable our ability to flourish. They are rooted in economic theory, which tells us that we must have a competitive advantage to survive and prosper in a universe of winners and losers. Behind the theory lies a deeply pessimistic view of essentially selfish human nature; a scramble for success in which it is us against the world. Here we look to a contrasting view of human nature which recognizes our self-centred drives, but which also points to a better way. This is the philosophy of the Buddha. Translated into our contemporary organizational context, Buddhist philosophy prioritizes the creation of value rather than capturing it; the development of an ecosystem of collaborative behaviour as opposed to an adversarial egosystem; and the ability to thrive under uncertainty rather than strive to control the future.

Chapter 4 is about creativity and critical thinking. Leaders often encourage the led – and themselves – to rely on common sense when in doubt about a course of action. Contemporary strategy, as discussed in the preceding chapter, is an example of this; surely, many leaders will say, it is common sense to view our organization as pitched in a struggle against the world. Here, we offer a provocative challenge to common sense as we introduce you to Karl Popper, a leading 20th-century philosopher. With Popper, we invite you to be critical rationalists. Of course, all ideas and proposals need critical challenge. However, Popper tells us, the idea or proposal that is most worthy of consideration is the idea that to the eye of common sense appears to be the least probable, but which can still stand up to criticism. In this chapter we use Popper's insight to stand conventional leadership wisdom on its head. We will show you how great outcomes are not so much a return on alignment and performance culture, as a return on truth, discovery and a learning culture. Results do not come from best practices but rather from unique practices, from embracing error as opposed to avoiding error. We will leave you with practical guidance on how to develop and experiment with critical insight in your own organization.

What would it be like if leaders set an example through their behaviour rather than set direction through their instructions? What if instead of dictating what is fair, leaders asked the question, what is fair? In Chapter 5, we invite you to step into a thought experiment, the veil of ignorance, devised by 20th-century American philosopher John Rawls – an experiment in which the rules of the game are agreed without the rule makers knowing their position in the game. But first we explore with the help of Ancient Greek philosopher Plutarch the power of the leader as an exemplar. We explore how the way a leader behaves, what they spend their time on and who they spend it with reveals their character. We see that it is a virtuous character that others are inspired by and the absence of virtues in our leaders that adds to our sense of alienation.

Our misguided approach to empowerment is the focus of Chapter 6. Empowerment has become a mantra in organizational life. Ironically, the approach taken to empowerment in many organizations is a direct cause of powerlessness and a reinforcer of alienation – the sickness that we seek to treat in this book. The mistake is the failure to understand where power comes from. It does not come from leaders, it comes from the led. Here we draw on the insight of the 17th-century English philosopher Thomas Hobbes. Hobbes saw that the authority of the king, for all his apparent might, was completely dependent on the way in which others had delegated their own authority upwards, in order to ensure a peaceful society in which all could flourish. In this chapter, we build on Hobbes' argument with the help of 18th-century philosopher Immanuel Kant to show that leadership is about opening up space in which individuals can act autonomously, bound by a duty to others. Here, your role as leader is to exemplify what duty to others means in the context of your organization's purpose. Remember: authority is a gift bestowed on you by others. It can be taken away, leaving you with only an impressive business card.

In organizations that have grown beyond a handful of people, leaders look to communication as a means of getting things done. In Chapter 7, we will see how communication has become one way. The problem is that communicating has become confused with telling. The sad reality is that the action you want to see happen does not necessarily follow from what you have told people to do. In exploring why we continue to pursue this telling approach, we draw on the stoic philosopher Epictetus of the first century AD, who opened our eyes to the fact that some things are uncontrollable and that attempting to control them can only lead to unnecessary pain. Seen in this light, leaders should realize that they cannot control how people respond to new information. Building on Epictetus' insight, we turn to David Hume, a famous Scottish philosopher of the 18th century, who shows that the most important responses to what people hear are in the heart rather than the head. Leaders need to facilitate the space for meaning to be made and indeed, the most important communication is from the led to the leader rather than the other way around.

Chapter 7 focuses on meaningful communication – here we ask whether we are looking to learn, or simply to convince; in Chapter 8 we turn to a closely related topic: engagement. Just as leaders invest heavily in telling people what to do, they also seek 'buy-in'. In this chapter, we focus on the relationship between leader and led and find that the very idea of engagement stands in the way of humanizing our workplace. Our insights come from the 20th-century philosopher Martin Buber, who asks us how we are making contact with others. One option is depersonalized, and very prevalent in organizational life: this is the I-It relationship, in which others are instruments of our will – acknowledged through submission or 'buy-in' – so that the right things can happen. The other option is what Buber describes as the I-Thou relationship, in which we are meeting and encountering others as fully fledged persons rather than transacting with them instrumentally. It is the leader who needs to engage by creating a meaningful encounter, rather than the led.

In Chapter 9 we turn to values. Today, the leaders in any organization are expected to produce a list of virtues: integrity, customer-centricity, entrepreneurialism – and so the list goes on and on. In general, we believe that these are well-meaning attempts to define goodness in organizational life. But, as leaders and led well know, for the most part the recitations of corporate values arouse cynical yawns. Even Enron had a set of corporate values, with integrity at the top of the list. In this chapter, the crucial insight that we offer is that there is no single model of the good life; no single set of values of equal relevance to everyone in your organization. Individuals have values, organizations do not. Individuals' values are shaped from infancy to adulthood and do not change due to an organization's values programme. We will draw on the insights of the great 20th-century philosopher Isaiah Berlin, one of the foremost advocates of pluralism. Guided by Berlin, we will show you how there are multiple interpretations of the good life, and how they are often at odds with each other. As leaders, we should not fall back on a hymn sheet of values. Rather, we will show you how to develop a moral compass that will help you to argue courageously and choose your course of action when confronted by the dilemmas of conflicting versions of the good.

Finally, Chapter 10 puts a spotlight on the leader herself. A flourishing individual is someone who has the freedom to choose. But what do we do when our freely made choices go wrong? Some leaders may let themselves off the hook by claiming extenuating circumstances or even that they had no choice in the first place. That, however, ignores the proper constraint on our freedom, which is self-imposed, so also freely chosen. As free people, we willingly accept rules and the consequences of breaking them. We can rejoice in the successes that we attribute to our actions, but we must also take responsibility for our failures; not to do so is to deny our humanity. Socrates tells us that spiritedness or protecting our honour is a defining human characteristic, and the last thing that we should give up. This sets us a challenge: what do you stand for as a leader that goes beyond your self-interest, your fears and your desires?

This book is a call to action, whatever your role in the workplace. We have a duty to make it more human for both others and ourselves.

We recognize that our readers will approach this book from different places.

One of our colleagues, for example, told us that while he would read the book because he liked philosophy, he didn't feel in the least alienated. For him there was some drudgery in the workplace, of course, but by and large he felt that he had great freedom to pick and choose, come and go and express himself in a way that others valued highly too. Here we have a warning – will those favourable conditions last? Will his attitude towards them last? What we propose in this book will help make the fulfilment that you might already experience more sustainable.

A friend, who read up to this point with a draft of the book, got really annoyed. 'Of course, I'm alienated,' she said. 'Who wouldn't be when they can do nothing to change the so-called working environment, which means the greedy, unhelpful people I'm stuck with every day. The best I can do is to put in the hours, take their money and hope I have the energy to flourish for five minutes in the evening with a strong gin and tonic.'

> While it may seem a tall order, even if we cannot change internal conditions, we may – with what this book proposes – be able to change how we respond to them.

John, the doorman at the London head office of one of the Big Four accounting firms, had a tightly circumscribed security role, but also an uncanny ability to remember names and engage authentically with visitors as they came and went. The managing partner told us that John had salvaged many a client situation where senior professional staff had struggled. Every year, they took him to Davos to be doorman at the entrance to their tent. John was no cog in a machine.

If you can't change the constraints you can, to a degree, change yourself. Indeed, the constraints may be the key to finding out how we want to change – to revealing our dreams.

Note

1 Marx, K (1814) The economic and philosophical manuscripts of 1841, in *Karl Marx, Early Writings*, trans T B Bottomore, McGraw Hill, 1963

01

Who can reconnect us with our dreams?

Your dream job and funeral eulogy

In one of our degree programmes, we ask our mature students to write a short description of their dream job following graduation, and why they are the perfect candidate for that job. The students are typically in mid-career, with a realistic appraisal of the opportunities around them as well as the spark of ambition that drew them back into the world of studying. The dream jobs generally fall into the well-recognized categories of business functions: marketing, business development, finance and the like. Job titles are mostly conventional – Vice President of this, Director of that – and money is often mentioned, not surprisingly given the educational debts that students are starting to incur as they embark on the assignment. Typically, the qualifications students give for those dream jobs are lists of promotions and other kinds of recognition by others over the prior years. 'Now I've written it down,' said one student, 'it doesn't sound like much of a dream and what I did to get there sounds really boring!'

But she had not at that point learned about the second part of the assignment. Once the dream jobs had been turned in, we asked our students to write a second short report. This rolled the clock forward some 40 years, and the task was to write down what their best friend would say about them at a poignant but celebratory occasion: their own funeral. And then they were invited to share and comment on both assignments with a fellow student. Was there a connection between the dream job and the funeral eulogy? What was the meaning of the connection, or lack of it? Which of the two assignments was more interesting and enjoyable to read? You could try out the two assignments yourself before reading on.

Invariably the eulogy stood out as being more passionate, more life affirming and more human. The account of the dream job, by contrast, was often colder, focused on the position and not the person. But it was usually a clear and structured account, whereas the eulogies, while inspiring, tended to be vague with rather generic hopes to lead a good life and make the world a better place. The two follow-up questions, spurring debate for the whole year ahead and far beyond, were these: what would it take to bring the aspirational flavour of the eulogy into the dream job and the workplace containing it? And what would it take to bring the rigour and realism of the dream job description into the eulogy?

Psychologists' advice about the good life

Psychologists claim that they have the answer to those two questions about our students' dream job and funeral eulogy.

In a tradition going back to the 1940s, humanists such as Abraham Maslow recognized the need to fulfil dreams in the workplace. Maslow talked about a hierarchy of needs, starting with food and shelter. While some people appear to need a great deal of food and shelter in the form of massive bonuses, Maslow argued that human beings need something else. Once material needs were met, they would be superseded by the need to communicate with others, to find and express an identity in the workplace, and finally to 'self-actualize', giving expression to the individual's fullest potential. This is, we are to hope, the space in which the dream job and the funeral eulogy find each other, and where Marx's ultimate challenge of alienation – alienation from one's own self – is finally resolved.

Over the last 70 years, business schools have gained influence and credibility, spawning a plethora of consulting firms, gurus and blockbuster managerial primers. Within that broadly defined world of business academia, psychology has become the dominant discipline. In most business schools today, Organizational Behaviour departments, filled with psychologists, tend to be the largest, overtaking finance and economics in numbers of professors, with the most PhD students and the lion's share of learning and development programmes in both university settings and the workplace. All our psychology colleagues would agree that their discipline – the study of the psyche after all – is there to help humans achieve their potential, and that managerial psychology should help them self-actualize in the workplace.

But what does it mean, to realize your fullest potential? What does it mean, as Maslow put it, to be self-actualized? How would you know? Cognitive psychologists, who tend to proliferate in academic institutions, would tell us that the answer is simple: go out and ask people if they are flourishing. As a result, countless survey instruments, questionnaires and self-raters are deployed to gauge workplace engagement, flourishing and self-actualization. The further promise is that the data will make the workplace better by homing in on those conditions that appear to yield the higher scores. But sadly, in practice, the engagement surveys primarily serve to generate peak levels of anxiety in Human Resource departments when numerical rankings start to slide despite hugely expensive interventions designed to help people feel better in the workplace.

Believing in this approach to self-actualization, the central Human Resources department of one of our clients, a huge global bank, developed a programme to help several thousand middle managers become more 'emotionally engaged' with executing the organization's strategy. The strategy itself was not a promising start, being a collage of worthy exhortations to 'customer-centricity' and an 'innovation culture'. But the grumblings in the pilot session turned into open dissent when the trainers ran a workshop designed to make participants feel empowered to act on their own initiative and feel personal ownership of the bank's projects. Trainers had asked them to work in small groups to remember a time when they felt empowered. Nobody mentioned the workplace. One manager in the group that we observed spoke of time spent coaching his children's sports classes; another talked about fundraising for the mosque. The trainer then asked them to imagine that they were enjoying the same feelings of empowerment as they went about their duties for the bank. 'But why,' said one, 'are you asking us to feel empowered here when we are clearly not?' The trainer, summoning up dwindling reserves of geniality, talked about the need for what she called 'buy-in'. 'That's even worse – an insult to our intelligence. These sessions are compulsory. To talk of buying in to the company's strategy and training programmes says that we are like customers and have a choice when it comes to what's on offer – obviously we don't. But we don't need to be sold to. We just need to have our intelligence respected and not be fed these Soviet-era slogans.' Subsequently we learned that the HR department had mandated a new programme of mindfulness-based stress management for all employees.

Let's be clear. The HR department meant well. There was no intention to insult employees. They genuinely wanted people to feel better. But here lies a fundamental flaw that takes us to the heart of this book.

> Feeling empowered is not the same as being empowered. Feeling engaged and self-actualized, or more self-actualized than yesterday, is not the same as self-actualization.

My feeling that I am flourishing – which I reported on a numerical scale in that engagement survey – can be an unreliable indicator of whether I am really flourishing. Feeling good is not necessarily the same as leading the good life.

What's wrong with feeling good?

Nothing – but don't rely on that as the litmus test of self-actualization. For – as we now go on to show – there is a fundamental weakness in the psychological perspective.

Psychologists hold that feeling good or happy, living the good life, can be understood through scientific methods, as it is deemed measurable (by self-reported scores) and its enablers can supposedly be discovered through statistical analysis of large data samples or through repeatable experiments.

This view of the good life is dominant in contemporary academic and business literature. It includes theories about what drives our emotional states, explaining psychic flourishing as the opposite of depression and anxiety. Daniel Haybron, who studies the science of happiness, cites three kinds of states. The first are what he calls *endorsement* states: emotions like joy or sadness, which endorse the conditions of life around someone. The second are *engagement* states, such as feelings of flow or vitality in relation to the world, and the third are *attunement* states, such as tranquillity, emotional expansiveness and confidence. But these supposedly scientific approaches face some big challenges.

The first is that there may not be much we can do to change our feelings. This is expressed in set point theory: the idea that everyone has an enduring set point for feeling good, a certain individual propensity to be more or less happy, to which each of us will regress over time, regardless of what we do or have done to them. Studies have assessed the impact of severe physical trauma, bereavement, divorce, financial loss and moving to a new house. These hurt. But within a year or so, people tend to revert to their earlier feelings about themselves and the world. Some studies point to collective set points, in which most people in a given culture report similar and stable levels of happiness. Other studies locate the set point in heredity, showing that separated twins report similar affect.

A second challenge is to do with the limitations of reports. Richard Feldman, President of the University of Rochester in New York State, points out that survey data about affect – or feeling – suffers from perceptions being unreliably grounded.[1] He refers to the instability problem (perception may change); the lability problem (perceptions may be affected by trivial factors, such as an attractive interviewer); and the timing problem (there is no ideal moment to report how good one feels, deathbed retrospection being especially unreliable). Martha Nussbaum, a law and philosophy professor at the University of Chicago, also describes a bullying problem: psychologists unwittingly bully their subjects into rating how they feel on a very limited range of measures or even a single scale, whereas, intuitively, feeling good should refer to multiple determinants.[2]

The third challenge is that our ability to perceive our own feelings may change over time. If our ability deteriorates, then we might simply be leading an impoverished and stunted life in which we are overly thankful for small mercies.

But there are even more fundamental challenges to the view that the good life is about good feelings. Writing in 1974, the philosopher Robert Nozick offered his 'pleasure machine' (or 'experience machine') as a thought experiment.[3] The pleasure machine can offer indefinite feelings of pleasure of any kind, from hedonic and emotional states to whole-life satisfaction. But, he asserts, few would choose this option, because of the intuition that these enjoyable states must be earned through activity. Martha Nussbaum went on to contrast her acquaintances leading a pleasant contemplative life with those leading an activist life of great achievement at the expense of stress, health and isolation, and she argues that most people would judge the latter as better off.

Doing what's good for you

Psychologists see the good life as feeling good. But are you doing what's good for you?

A subjective answer – simply doing what you want, getting what you want and wanting what you get – is not good enough. For example, you might want to spend a life counting leaves all day long, which intuitively would not seem to count as a good life. As well as the challenge of weird ambition, subjective answers to the question 'What's good for me?' are vulnerable to low ambition; realizing a desire to live doing little or nothing would again, intuitively, seem to fall short of a good life. And desire might take the form of destructive goals; Attila the Hun may well have wanted what he got (except for choking to death on a nosebleed on his wedding night). These challenges point to the need for a more objective answer to questions about what is good for you.

Martin Seligman, founder of the positive psychology tradition, takes the notion of the good life away from feelings and subjectivity towards a list of worthwhile pursuits.[4] The list could include career success, friendship, art appreciation, achieving an MA in philosophy and so on. Here, the problem is that although any of these pursuits might intuitively seem to be worthwhile, it is not clear how they should be ranked. That is important, because greater degrees of flourishing should result from engaging in more valuable pursuits. There needs to be an objective basis for ranking them a 'good-maker' without which subjectivity is bound to return.

How do we find that 'good-maker', an objective means for deciding whether achieving an MBA at a business school trumps art classes or vice versa?

> While psychology with its research tools can help us to understand our positive or negative feelings, we need to tap another source of wisdom to understand what is good for us and hence can help make a good workplace.

Philosophy is that source – for philosophers have sought over millennia to understand what it means to flourish, what is good for us, so that we can realize our fullest potential.

Let us turn to two philosophers who have strong views about the 'good-maker', the criteria by which we judge something to be better for us and others than something else. We go on to consider how the workplace would be designed in either case to enable the good, flourishing human life. Our first sage is Aristotle, who taught two-and-a-half millennia ago. Our second stands at the beginning of the postmodern era: the German philosopher Friedrich Nietzsche. The preoccupation of both is with what it takes to be fully human: a person rather than an animal, a slave or a member of the herd. Both look to help us discover objective answers with far-ranging implications for all aspects of life, not least how we work. For Aristotle, being fully human means being – and allowing others to be – reasonable. Reason is his 'good-maker': the more reasonable the better. For Nietzsche, the 'good-maker' is excellence, passionately expressed.

Summary

Before we introduce you to Aristotle and Nietzsche in Chapter 2, we remind you that in this chapter we explored psychology's response to the challenge of flourishing as opposed to workplace alienation. We found that response limited by reliance on empirical data, which in turn derives from reported feelings about flourishing, rather than flourishing itself. Doing what's good for you does not always feel good. Philosophy claims to look beyond feelings into the fundamentals of flourishing.

Questions

1 How would you describe your dream job and the eulogy that your best friend would give at your funeral? Is there a connection between the two? If so, what is the meaning of that connection? If there is no connection, does that matter?

2 Are you and your subordinates at work flourishing? How would you know?

3 What have you achieved that you now take pride in, where you had doubts and made difficult sacrifices at the time?

Notes

1 Feldman, R (2008) Whole life concepts of happiness, *Theoria*, **74** (3),
   pp. 219–38
2 Nussbaum, M (2012) Who is the happy warrior? Philosophy, happiness,
   research and public policy, *International Review of Economics,* **59**, pp. 335–61
3 Nozick, R (1974) *Anarchy, State and Utopia*, Basic Books, New York,
   pp. 42–45
4 Seligman, M E P (2002) *Authentic Happiness*, Free Press, New York

02

Reason and passion in the humanized workplace

Who was Aristotle?

One of our colleagues mocked our project of drawing on ancient wisdom for contemporary insight, saying:

> Philosophers were all white, male, lived weird lives – usually alone –
> far removed from the concerns of ordinary people. And they are long
> dead. What can you possibly take from them in today's world in
> which we have real, live, empirical science rather than old memories
> of star-gazing?

Aristotle lived long ago (c 384 to c 322 BCE) and was male, but otherwise did not fit that bill. He would have been brown rather than white, loved women, founded and managed the Lyceum (his own learning institute), became tutor to Alexander the Great and had interests ranging from marine biology through meteorology to the art of leadership. This extraordinary polymath enrolled in Plato's Academy in Athens at the age of 17 following the lineage of Socrates, later departing radically from his teachers to develop his own point of view. That point of view later led him to flee Athens on capital charges of mocking the gods. For developing a point of view is at the heart of Aristotle's own teaching.

Only a small proportion of Aristotle's written works survives, preserved by Islamic civilization. Much of his writing explores what it means to be fully human. For our purposes, the most insightful account is to be found in *Nicomachean Ethics*, in which Aristotle asks what distinguishes a person – a fully fledged human being – from an animal or a slave. Animals are driven by raw passion and appetite; slaves are simply driven by others, with no power of their own. Neither of those two conditions allow for happiness and flourishing.

> The slave has no freedom to make choices; animals live a life red in tooth and claw and suffer greatly in consequence. A flourishing person, by contrast, is someone who learns what is good for him or her and has the freedom to choose accordingly.

The distinguishing human quality that makes that possible is reason, which animals do not have, and which slaves cannot use. Reason is the 'good-maker', which guides us on what to do with the challenges and opportunities that life brings us.

Aristotle's middle way

Aristotle took the view that 'virtues' – which make for a life well lived – are pretty obvious. For him, they included friendship, generosity, courage and resilience. His list from nearly 2,500 years ago still makes intuitive sense today. But without context, they are meaningless. Courage sounds good, but is only a word unless we know what it means in a given situation. Here Aristotle urges us to discover what he calls 'the middle way'. This is the middle way between the 'vice' of excess or deficiency; going too far or not far enough. So, the virtue of courage lies somewhere between the vice of excess – rashness – and the vice of deficiency, which is cowardice. Similarly, no good friend is constantly flattering you and trying to please; nor is a good friend always prickly and critical. Great friendship is found somewhere between the two. Similarly, generosity is to be found somewhere between throwing your money away and being a miser. In the world of work, Aristotle's sweet spot – between being a bully on the one hand and a weakling on the other – is being a tough, resilient person.

But how do we discover that sweet spot? Aristotle's answer is that we discover it by using our reason, honed by education: exploring how we and others might act in given situations, carrying out experiments, reflecting on the outcome and trying again. There is also an obligation for those who have learned to use reason to teach others, so that they too can find the middle way. In Aristotle's time – and today – the world was very volatile, uncertain, complex and ambiguous. Simply following the rules or doing what we have always done or feel like doing will not serve us well. We have to develop our own point of view if we are to count as fully fledged human beings.

Aristotle's ideal workplace would be one in which we develop our humanity through opportunity and training to use our reason.

A workplace for slaves?

Aristotle would have liked the contemporary language of 'empowerment' but would then have had second thoughts on how that actually unfolds in many of our workplaces. One of us worked with a CEO who memorably said that for him 'the best managers are those in their late 30s with a large mortgage and several children'. In other words, they will do as they are told. We have worked with a large IT company whose salespeople are told again and again to 'get the numbers up this quarter come what may'. They all know that this will be at the cost of damaging customer relationships, but shrug and tell us that they are just following orders. One of our university colleagues – described as 'staff' rather than as 'faculty' in the strange hierarchy of academic life – pointed out anomalies in student grading systems and was told by a senior professor that he had no right to ask questions.

Aristotle would see this as modern slavery. Reasoned judgement shuts down. And that can be infectious. Irving Janis, a leading scholar at Yale University, coined the term 'groupthink' to describe a situation in which all members of a group go along with a course of action with which they all privately disagree, but never voice their disagreement.[1] A friend who was on the board of Barings, a blue-chip British investment bank that failed spectacularly in the mid-1990s, told us that everyone in the crucial board meeting wanted to ask the same question about the unusual trading results from the Singapore operation but failed to do so, not wanting to look foolish in the eyes of a dominant chairman. *Rogue Trader* was the name of the movie made about the bank's collapse, but an alternative title might have been *Lemmings Take Charge*. Slaves, like lemmings, will march to the cliffs if that is company policy.

Aristotle would not have encouraged trouble making and rule breaking for the sake of it. Far from it; he saw individuals acting as persons in the context of a community. His audience at the Lyceum was made up of free citizens who had an obligation to defend Athens, their city.

> That meant being committed to having a point of view – to have worked things out for oneself – but then respecting others' points of view and learning from them.

One professional services firm with which we work speaks of an 'obligation to dissent' for even its most junior professional staff. Once spoken, some dissenting views will undoubtedly have to be set aside for the sake of aligned action, but the quality of decision making will have been hugely enhanced. Those who have a point of view are also more likely to be reliable in troubled times. Slaves are more likely to panic and run, especially when the chain of command has been broken and no orders arrive.

A workplace for animals?

Slaves are not allowed to use or develop their reason; animals don't have it and act on instinct and passion.

Go to a trading floor and you will find those who are today some of the least respected people in the business community. In fairness, the traders we personally know best – in stocks, bonds, currencies or commodities – are eminently reasonable, have many opportunities to choose between right and wrong and look to do the right thing for themselves, their institutions and their clients.

Animal spirits can, however, take over. Famously, the world saw how traders at Enron gamed power supply in California, deliberately generating power shortages to create price spikes and thence super-normal profits. They did so with ever-increasing exuberance and glee, as recordings of the Enron traders attest. People died in 2001 when the Californian electricity network crashed in consequence: an operating theatre table was not a great place to be. But animal spirits, devoid of a moral compass, are not just the preserve of traders. A colleague in another institution gave us a video tape of Jeff Skilling, Enron's CEO, talking to MBA students at the time of those power outages. He began his speech with a big grin on his face and a joke. 'What's the difference,' he asked, 'between California and the Titanic?' His answer: 'At least when the Titanic went down the lights were on!' It is hard to think of a more tasteless joke about the toll of human suffering unleashed by his own traders. Soon after, Enron collapsed and Jeff Skilling was given a hefty prison sentence for fraud. But what struck us with dismay, as we viewed the video, was not the circumstances or the joke itself so much as the gales of laughter and rapturous applause from several hundred MBA students (not our own, we assure you) destined to become leaders. Animal spirits are contagious, and at times deadly.

> Here you might reflect on when you have seen animal spirits take over judgement in your own organization. And have you ever allowed immediate gratification to take over your own judgement?

For Aristotle, the issue would not have been the violation of some fixed moral code. Indeed, Aristotle would no doubt have imagined circumstances in which practical reason would have made the bank's financial health the top priority. The issue is that when animal spirits take over, it is the moral compass – not just the rules – that gets lost, and with that, the skill to decide on the right thing will get forgotten. One of our clients, who had just taken on the leadership of a major professional services firm, began his term of office by telling all those working in the organization that they must henceforth 'do the right thing'. We urged him to also invite his staff members to reflect on what doing the wrong thing might be, and what might make it so attractive, and where the grey areas between right and wrong might lie – for example in a questionably costly client entertainment. The challenge was not to lay down a moral code, but to help people develop a moral compass, powered by reason.

So, for Aristotle, humanizing the workplace means creating a more and more reasonable environment.

Nietzsche takes us beyond reason

With Nietzsche we catapult nearly two-and-a-half thousand years to the late 19th century. Nietzsche disagreed with almost everyone. He would have found Aristotle's reasonable workplace dreary, with everyone musing about the right thing to do rather than getting on with outstanding work and honing their skills to perfection. And yet he is very much in the lineage of Aristotle, addressing the same core question: what is the good life? Like Aristotle, he looks for an objective answer: feeling good is not enough. And like Aristotle he looks for a 'good-maker': a yardstick that allows us to figure out what is best, not blindly adopting others' moral codes or waiting for divine guidance that will never arrive.

In this book we will invite you into a range of 'what if' thought experiments: what if we organized our workplace and informed our behaviour based on a series of different philosophical insights about what makes for a good, fully human life? We began with Aristotle. We chose Nietzsche as our second guide in this opening chapter because he is poetic, extreme and controversial: as different as we could find from the cool, thoughtful, structured Aristotelian world view. By stepping into these two hugely different points of view on the good life from the beginning, we hope that your 'what if' curiosity will be stirred and that this will take you through our subsequent chapters with a questioning mind.

> We do not tell you to reorganize your workplace on Aristotelian, Nietzschean or any other lines but we do insist that you develop your own point of view: a point on which both Nietzsche and Aristotle would have agreed.

Nietzsche was born in Germany in 1844. His short but remarkable career ended with a mental collapse at the age of 45, from which he never recovered until his death in 1900. He influenced philosophers including Heidegger, Derrida and Foucault and had a huge impact on Carl Jung and Sigmund Freud, the founders of psychiatry. In literature, figures like Sartre, Camus, Thomas Mann and Herman Hesse owe part of their inspiration to him. On the darker side, aspects of his work were taken up by the Nazis in the 1920s and '30s, and his sister became a well-known admirer of Adolf Hitler. Grossly unfairly, those associations have come to dominate his perception in popular understanding. Grossly unfairly, because Nietzsche would have hated nothing more than ranks of sweaty men marching together in uniform, desperate to conform, shouting anti-Semitic or any other slogans and carrying flags. For mass movements of Nazis or any other groups would have represented precisely what he abhorred – the herd, in which much of humanity is trapped – and his teachings are all about how to rise beyond the herd and flourish as an individual.

For Nietzsche, to flourish as individuals – becoming Higher Men, as he describes those who have reached their full human potential – we must make our own judgements about the good life from our own experience. By contrast, members of the herd look to others to make their judgements for them. Those other might be priests, bosses or even philosophers. Even more perniciously, he argued, in Western culture at least, those who proclaimed the truth had encouraged a slave morality for the herd to follow. Here lay his famous attack on Christianity. Christianity, he alleged, arose as a religion among Roman slaves. While slaves in their heart of hearts wanted goods like wealth, power, beauty, joy and health, they knew they could never have them. So, their priests inverted noble standards of goodness – elevating meekness, altruism, humility, pity and patience – as revenge on the great, undermining individual flourishing so that even potentially great people might be seduced into abandoning their potential. At the same time, members of the herd would have some level of awareness of the good things they were rejecting, and their lives would be over-shadowed by a dull resentment, especially at those who appeared to be flourishing.

Have you ever seen this in your own workplace? Those in power speak of values and even commission consultants to run workshops so that all employees know what values they are meant to uphold. Typically, they say little about individual flourishing and a lot about teamwork, humility, compliance and engagement. Meanwhile, every-one knows very well that those who get to the top exhibit few of those qualities, but as good employees they attend the values classes nonetheless. Often, the only way in which resentment gets formalized is through the poor course evaluations given to the learning and development department. Hugh, a former colleague, told us of a corporate ethics initiative in which all senior staff had to sign an undertaking not to engage in corrupt activity, as a personal commit-ment to the CEO. 'He's making us cover his back', Hugh said. 'Of course, I'll sign it like everyone else. But he expects us to meet our numbers any way we can.' Interestingly, his boss – Sir Peter – told us that he detested corruption of any kind and thought it perfectly reasonable to expect all his subordinates to act on the oath he sent out even at the expense of meeting budget targets. His own values, alas, meant little if simply imposed on others.

The end of moral authority

In his own time Nietzsche saw a collapse of conventional moral authority, which made it imperative for people to discover their own values. The received wisdom of the Church, State and other institutions holding moral authority was increasingly coming into question, opening up the threat of nihilism – the conviction that life is meaningless. Nietzsche saw this as a cause of the collapse of the Western civilization of his era, which would lead at an individual level to cynicism, hedonism and despair – and at a collective level risk social breakdown and conflict. He wasn't far wrong. Not long after his death began the cycle of the most terrible wars that the world had ever seen, which still casts a long shadow over all our lives.

In many organizations today, we often see a collapse in trust and acceptance of authority, leading to cynicism and apathy. It's hard to see moral authority being restored in our organizations in an age where every opinion gets broadcast and any alleged misdeed of our leaders gets immediate exposure. All CEOs should explore Glassdoor to see what their employees really think of them, and not rely on the official engagement surveys. If people will no longer swallow others' values, then they must discover their own. And if your organization can make that a fundamental aspect of its purpose – helping people to discover and live out what they care about – then that in itself becomes an authentic collective value that can align action and release the extraordinary energy of a community of individuals rather than a demoralized herd.

Breaking away from the herd

Nietzsche gives a call to arms: to reinvent our own values. How do we do that? He tells us the key is self-awareness: awareness of the many levels of motivation, or drives, that govern our behaviour, and how we dress those drives up as values. We might take pride in our willingness to help others, for example. On examination, it might turn out that this arose from not wanting to disappoint our mother. There is nothing inherently wrong in that, but the mistake is to mask who we are with a set of values that belong to someone else. Nietzsche would encourage us to experiment, choosing which drives to let off the leash, seeing where that takes us, and if that is to a place in which we are more invigorated, less resentful, more potent and proud of ourselves – exercising what he called 'the will to power' – then we can attach the label of values to the underlying drives. They will then be our own values, which will give us more insight into how we act and reflect on how we can act even better. Some of those drives will come from dark places but with awareness can be transformed: the impetus to cruelty, for instance, can be sublimated into competition for excellence. But if we continued to fool ourselves with the value of humility, then cruelty would remain a hidden drive with bad consequences, and the opportunity for excellence would drift by.

Life as a work of art

Nietzsche told us that we must take personal responsibility for who we are and what we do. That way, we will be crafting our lives and what we stand for, as an artist creates a masterpiece.

> Famously, Nietzsche invited us to imagine that a demon appeared before us one night and told us that our lives would be repeated again and again, endlessly, with every pain, sorrow, joy, pleasure, achievement and humiliation. Would we curse the demon? Or would we feel immense gratitude because we were being allowed to endlessly experience our own creation, for good or ill? This was his litmus test of affirmation and responsibility for one's life.

Hand in hand with this cosmic level of personal responsibility, in Nietzsche's later work he urged us to pay attention to the 'little things' – diet, exercise, sunlight, moments of rest – for he also saw it as our duty to be sufficiently resilient to take on responsibility for our lives.

For Nietzsche, living responsibly is a life of struggle. Many of his metaphors are of mountain climbing: embracing effort and discarding ease on the ascent to master the summit. Indeed, he wrote many of his works in a chalet overlooking the Engadine in the Swiss Alps. His Higher Man is hard on himself, self-disciplined, and associates only with his peers who can encourage and challenge him on the climb. It is not all hard grind, because his Higher Man will laugh and leap for joy on the mountain top, but that is not a reward, simply part of being creative. The Higher Man who has escaped from the herd and slave morality will be dedicated to a great creative work that unifies his energy and skill: an 'organizing idea' that becomes his life's purpose.

The Nietzschean workplace

Would you hire one of Nietzsche's Higher Men? This would be a difficult, unreasonable person, not suited to bureaucratic processes but one who would bring incredible creative determination to your organization. Probably you have them on the payroll already. If your HR department can tolerate them skipping those values workshops, they may survive to become your most important people assets, probably as individual contributors rather than as managers or managed. But will they stay with you?

Many organizations have 360-degree surveys in which people are evaluated by their colleagues, bosses and subordinates. Often those evaluations are tied to bonuses and promotions. We can easily imagine that process being anathema to any self-respecting Nietzschean, for the judgement about what is good, and whether work has been well done belongs only to those who have developed the capacity to make that judgement: true peers whose judgement the Nietzschean respects. A herd judgement can only lead to the exit door.

Nietzscheans look to develop, hence the plentiful mountain-climbing imagery. Just doing a job is a turn-off. Instead we would help those aspirant Higher Men to create their own development plans, recognizing that this would encompass life outside the workplace and indeed a career beyond you, their current employer.

Rather than placing our Nietzscheans in teams, we would enable them to find their peers and form networks with others on the upward path, who are pursuing a diverse range of creative work and want to share challenges and inspiration.

Like Nietzsche himself, aspirant Higher Men are likely to live and work under immense strain, and just as Nietzsche spoke of the 'little things', the right environment – work space, views of nature, nourishing meals rather than pot noodles, and some more or less compulsory relaxation – will also be a key to retaining your Nietzschean talent.

Nietzsche urged the creation of good psychological – as well as physical – conditions as a key to flourishing. He gave two prescriptions. The first is to 'react as infrequently as possible'. He gives the examples of writers who ruin their genius by spending time and energy reacting to other people's ideas. 'Criticizing what other people have already thought,' he says, 'they do not think for themselves anymore.'[2] His second prescription is to be selfish – but in a qualified manner. He tells us to 'say No when to say Yes would be selfless, but also to say No as rarely as possible'. In other words, we should avoid situations that drain our psychological resources: paying attention to those little things avoids distraction from the great things, and conserves energy for the greater task. In our workplace we all know how energy gets leached away as one group of people reviews another group of people's projects, how we all hear the endless call for pointless collaboration that distracts us from our proper work, how we get drawn into those incessant email trails that never needed to have us copied in. The Nietzschean workplace would be designed to protect us from clutter and mess – from the hurry sickness that we described at the opening of this chapter.

Recently Sir Martin Sorrell spoke to our students about his new venture, founded after he left WPP in 2018. Sir Martin had built up WPP over 35 years as one of the three principal global holding companies in advertising and marketing services. Within WPP's agencies – Kantor, Ogilvy, J Walter Thompson and many more – are outstanding creative minds. But as Sir Martin told us, between those creative minds and the execution of their ideas were many enervating steps and processes which accumulated over time. Client managers would speak to clients, review the brief, planners would draft a strategy, mood and storyboards would iterate between different departments, the production team might query feasibility, and at the end the client might tell the WPP agency to start over. Even without trying to integrate disciplines across WPP companies the process could take months, with little scope for evaluating impact once the TV commercial had gone live. No wonder that advertising creatives liked to focus – as far as possible – on winning the Lions Awards for the best creative work at the Cannes Festival, where they would find real peer appreciation for their work outside the corporate quagmire.

Sir Martin's new business is S4 Capital. It sets creatives free of the old bureaucracy that stood between them and the world. As a leader in his seventies who could pass for 15 years younger, Sir Martin is revitalizing their excitement in seeing their creative ideas have impact. S4 Capital is the mothership for tightly connected disciplines that provide end-to-end solutions in digital media. The product cycle is measured in days, not months. The creative outputs – and the creatives themselves – are constantly tested through vigorous experimentation (as is Sir Martin). But this is not hurry sickness, chasing after trivia. Rather, it is the freedom to fully engage in the work that really matters, working as an artist and throwing out all the redundant, energy-sapping activities that clutter many workplaces. On interviewing Sir Martin, we saw him as something of a Nietzschean himself: 'What I do,' says, 'is not just a job.' He told us that he had no intention to stop and vegetate. S4 Capital is already disrupting the world of the big marketing services holding companies.

On a very different scale, Lance Lee founded The Apprenticeshop in the small fishing town of Rockport, Maine, in the 1970s. Lance was inspired by Kurt Hahn, an early advocate of experiential education for the development of individuality, and founder of the adventure training Outward Bound movement in which Lance himself was closely involved. Lance has handed on The Apprenticeshop but remains a huge figure in the Rockport community. The Apprenticeshop teaches people from all walks of life and geographical origins how to build wooden boats and offers a community that keeps their skills up to the mark. These are clinker-built boats, which might well have been completely superseded by modern materials but for Lance's insight that wood was the material which permitted the greatest hands-on craft excellence in design and construction, and that the values of craft excellence could generate economic value for the boat builders as well as the glow of creative work well done. Lance not only ran a business and taught skills, he remains alight with passion for what he does in this remote location and has infected his apprentices with the same passion and confidence that they could gain mastery over the material and the elements. At the same time, Lance and his graduates had zero tolerance for slackness and failure to commit. His apprentices were equipped to make a worthwhile living as well, since boats made by the Apprenticeshop alumni are coveted by the wealthier sailors on the New England coast.

One of our friends and mentors, the late Sumantra Ghoshal of INSEAD and the London Business School, spoke of the 'smell of the place'. He recalled the forests of Fontainebleau around INSEAD in springtime, and how in the invigorating air he could not help but jog on the woodland paths, leaping to catch a branch, a song on his lips. By contrast, he told us of downtown Calcutta in August, where he returned each year for family reasons. There, the humidity, temperature, crowds and mess left him exhausted, on his bed for most of the day. 'Are we,' he asked in one of his lectures to a group of senior executives, 'creating in our organizations the forest of Fontainebleau, or downtown Calcutta in August?' Nietzscheans need the springtime. Sumantra himself was a Nietzschean. His test for bringing a new member into his department, whatever their discipline or training, was simply whether they were extraordinary.

Summary

In this chapter we have given you a taste of two philosophers who share a concern for human flourishing, but with two very different approaches and very different implications for the humanized workplace. Which are you drawn to? Is it the cool rationality of Aristotle? Or Nietzsche's passionate drive for excellence? And how far does your workplace allow you to develop in either direction?

Those questions raise a fundamental question. Can our organizations accommodate both aspirant Nietzscheans and followers of Aristotle's Middle Way? We believe that they must. Within your organization you will no doubt find arenas for bold experimentation and revitalization that need the Nietzschean spirit. In other situations, the call will be for stability, coordination and progressive improvement rather than revolutionary change – here the Aristotelians will thrive. The key is to avoid a one-size-fits-all approach to selecting people, measuring performance, offering rewards and shaping processes, so that we design the organization around the person rather than the other way around.

Questions

1 How much freedom do you have in your workplace? How far can you choose which activities to pursue? If you have little freedom to choose your tasks, how much inner freedom might you develop in the way you respond to those constraints?

2 Where do your ideas about the good life come from? To what extent are those ideas coming from your own judgement?

3 What is the 'organizing idea' that gives your organization purpose? What is the 'organizing idea' that gives purpose to your life and the lives of those in your care?

Notes

1 Janis, I L (1971) Groupthink, *Psychology Today*, 5 (6), pp. 43–46; 74–76
2 Nietzsche, F (1888) *Ecce Homo*, p. 95

03

Humanizing strategy

The rise of the strategist

In the last chapter we explored what it takes to flourish in an organization. Flourishing for Aristotle meant not being a slave or an animal and instead becoming more fully a person by developing our reason. For Nietzsche, flourishing meant not being a dumb member of the herd – instead standing out as what he called a 'Higher Man' by dint of excellence and passion. Either of those paths towards flourishing takes us further away from the state of alienation that Karl Marx decried – as we saw in the opening of this book – and further towards the humanized workplace.

The juxtaposition of two very different philosophers shows that there is no single path towards flourishing. That has crucial implications for both leaders and the led in our organizations. As the led, we need to understand and test what alternative paths allow our own individual flourishing. As leaders, we will need to open those different paths. In the humanized workplace, leaders are ultimately the custodians of human flourishing.

Typically, however, our leaders have more immediate preoccupations, being held accountable for both immediate performance and the longer-term strategic direction of the organization. In this chapter, we focus on strategy. Does strategy help or hinder the humanizing of the workplace? Can philosophy help make strategy better, in the sense of helping us to flourish?

Strategists have become the high priests of contemporary organizations. Within the world's leading business schools, professors in the strategy department are typically the pre-eminent faculty members, annoying their colleagues with their guru status and the impressive fees they can command from short keynote talks at management conferences in enviable five-star locations.

> Inside corporations and government departments, the strategy or policy team has huge influence and is often as seen a hothouse for nurturing the next generation of talent, accelerating it on a fast track to the top.

Within the world of management consulting, those who call themselves strategists command the highest day rates behind a cloak of mystique, claiming to be the 'trusted adviser' to the client's top management.

Some years back, we were told, one of the major audit firms acquired a strategy consulting boutique and sought to integrate it. The plan was to use those 'trusted adviser' relationships to sell in more mundane process improvement work – sadly, without success. It had been agreed to house the strategy consultants in the same building as the auditors to prompt cross-selling. And indeed, the move took place – but the design also called for a partition between the auditors and the strategists. Early on, somebody altered the design specification to include a communicating door between the two working areas. Soon the door became locked and the key was lost. On one side of the door, brown-coloured and brown-tasting lukewarm refreshments came out of a machine, paid for with tokens. On the other side of the door, a barista was employed to make perfect cappuccinos, with brain-enhancing high-end energy drinks available on tap. You will immediately guess on which side the strategy consultants were sitting.

One of us authors confessed to the rest that in his youth he had been employed by a leading strategy consulting house. His task, two years out of his MBA programme at a prestigious business school? To advise on a strategy for new rolling mills for a global aluminium company. His team laboured night and day for a month, producing ingenious economic analyses captured on PowerPoint. Then came the day to present to the company board, whose average age was roughly twice those of the consulting team members. The young team wowed the board, whose members came close to giving a standing ovation when a particularly compelling two-by-two matrix appeared on the screen, replete with circles and arrows. But, standing at the back of the room, our co-author was aware of a group of middle managers who seemed far from overjoyed. During the coffee break, one of them approached our co-author. 'I know,' he said, very quietly, 'that you know precisely nothing about aluminium rolling.' Our then youthful co-author felt the floor disappearing beneath him. But then this manager – a seasoned metallurgist and engineer – put a steadying hand on his shoulder. 'Don't worry,' he went on, softly, so nobody could overhear. 'I am going to teach you. My bosses obviously love your ideas. They will listen to you, not me, but I can at least make sure that your ideas have some connection to reality – and you can make sure that my project does not get lost.'

Strategy and inhumanity

Strategy and strategists have a very mixed reputation, notwithstanding those high fees, status and mystique.

Those on the receiving end of strategy in organizations typically groan when a new one is unveiled with endless slides. We met a middle manager who relieved the tedium by organizing a game of buzzword bingo during the annual strategy meeting in her organization. Her colleagues were surreptitiously handed worksheets with squares. In each square appeared a strategy buzzword such as 'core competence' or 'synergy'. As the speaker proceeded, every now and then a member of the audience would say 'Bingo!' The speaker was immensely flattered: the point had hit home. But it simply meant that somebody had completed a row or a column. 'I know it was childish,' she told us, 'but we all felt that we had entered a make-believe world.'

At the same time, everyone wants to be 'strategic'. We hear of those working in strategic purchasing, strategic selling, or strategic facilities management; developing human resource strategy, strategic information systems and executing endless strategic initiatives. That begs the question of what 'strategic' might mean. The inference is that it must mean something very important, presumably containing an idea that we want our colleagues and top management to recognize as relevant and interesting. And yet, as we saw in our short story about aluminium rolling, many of us at the same time doubt the connection between ideas and reality.

Strategy should be pretty straightforward. A good strategy describes what we want to become and how we are going to get there. It can apply at any level of life, from the affairs of a great corporation to an individual's personal development. What could be simpler? The complexity of course arises when we start to dig deeper into the end and the means, the what and the how.

> Inevitably we will make assumptions about the desirability of a given end and the feasibility of a given means. And it is here that we see a fundamental problem with strategy as commonly practised in organizations today. Its dominant ideas and assumptions are compelling, and at the same time deeply dehumanizing and detached from human reality.

We will explore why that should be the case, and promise to show you, a little later in the chapter, how we can lift the gloom when we introduce you to the insights of another philosopher, who precedes even Aristotle.

Think of your own organization. What is the end that your strategy drives towards? We would be amazed if you were not seeking success. What then makes that possible? We see that a dominant assumption has become universal throughout the corporate world, one which we see becoming widespread in the public sector and even in the world of charities and social enterprises. This is the proposition that success depends on a sustainable competitive advantage; that there will be winners and losers and that good strategy leads to winning, permanently if we can make it so. This lies in the roots of the word itself: in ancient Greek, 'strategos' translates as the military commander whose job is to crush the opposition. The idea that we should seek sustainable competitive advantage to succeed has become pervasive, like an organizational mantra. The word 'mantra' in its original Sanskrit means a magic spell, and this is one which can leave us spellbound in ways that rob us of our humanity.

The problem does not lie with competition, but rather the use to which we put it.

Is your strategy about capturing value from others – or creating it?

Competition itself is a contest, and by competing in any walk of life we become stronger and wiser as we learn from and seek to exceed the best. The difficulty lies with the idea of a sustainable advantage, implying that we are pitched against the world and need a position in which we are unassailable. For several decades, countless managers have been exposed to concepts derived from micro-economics, made popular by Michael Porter, a leading Harvard professor, that tell us that in an unassailable position we have enormous bargaining power.[1] That is, the power to drive down the price that our suppliers can charge us and drive up the price we charge our customers because they have nowhere else to go; the power to suppress competitors and block new entrants or substitutes from entering the markets that we control. The more power, so the argument goes, the greater our success, because of our ability to capture value – be it money or other kinds of resources and opportunities – from others. The irony, of course, is that a sustainable competitive advantage means the reverse of competition: ultimately it means creating a monopoly.

Underlying the view of competitive advantage as the driver of success is a view of humanity. Oliver Williamson, the 2009 Nobel Prize-winning economist, coined it succinctly when he described 'strategic behaviour' as 'the making of false threats and promises' on the premise that people are opportunistic, or 'self-interest seeking with guile'.[2] If that is how people are, then it follows that they will seek to overpower us in the bargaining contest, and we need a good strategy to secure our own power ahead of theirs, to create something as close to a monopoly as possible before they do. If the world is a harsh place, then we need a big stick to see off predators. The big stick is our competitive advantage or bargaining power. Here is a compelling idea that shapes strategy.

Where does it lead?

> Today, we see competition reducing in the technology world as major players consolidate their competitive advantage, creating oligopolies whose untrammelled power over our lives as well as our pockets is increasingly coming into question.

At their most extreme and intense, 'strategic behaviour' and 'competitive advantage' are to be found in the Mexican drug cartels or the post-Soviet kleptocracies. At least, some might say, those organizations that have secured a competitive advantage can use their power to provide their employees with better security, a more nurturing work environment and make more money at the same time. That might be true in stable environments: historically, firms like Unilever and Procter & Gamble, or SAP and Oracle, split markets between themselves, nothing much changed, and employee benefits were good (not necessarily for all in the business or supply chain). But in those conditions innovation suffers, and – for the most part – the scramble for greater bargaining power leads to beggar-my-neighbour tactics in which everyone is ultimately the loser. One of our co-authors, who supervises a family farming business in Argentina, was enlisted by a major national agricultural association to promote better coordination and cooperation between landowners, tenant farmers, contractors, transporters, animal feed companies, poultry producers and distributors – all the way through what is often described as the 'value chain', or the steps through which raw material passes to become a final product. Coordination and cooperation had been non-existent. Waste and delay crippled the sector, which should have been one of the world's most productive. Why should that be the case, our co-author enquired? The candid answer from all the players was this: we don't trust each other. Each feared that the other would seize advantage to drive an ever-harder bargain.

This root idea of contemporary strategy is so pervasive that our students find it impossible to shake off even when they know its consequences. We have been running a course on strategies for climate change and environmental sustainability, which typically attracts students who are more caring, less red in tooth and claw than most who sign up for an MBA programme. They believe that coordination and cooperation are essential if the major existential threats now facing humanity are to be addressed. But they nonetheless behave in surprising ways. We put them to the test by inviting them to take part in Fishbanks, a classic business simulation. Our students form several groups; each group is given a notional fishing company to run and its members can decide how many ships to buy, build and send out to sea. It soon becomes apparent that the largest fishing companies are making more money and a scramble for domination ensues. The game gets noisy and exciting and we typically raise the tempo by auctioning off additional ships, taking care to explain that these have just become available at auction because of the collapse of a fishery elsewhere in the world: a strong hint of what is to come. The bidding nonetheless quickly becomes a frenzy. The outcome? You guessed it. The players ruin the fishery. Often, a student will rise to her feet early in the game, pointing out the inevitable, pleading for a shared solution rather than each seeking to capture value independently. Typically, some but not all the groups will attempt to share information and develop common strategies, but it turns out that those who flout the collective endeavour are the ones that immediately make more money. Others then also break ranks – until the final collapse, which is a typical illustration of the 'tragedy of the commons'. Everyone depends on a shared resource, but it is in nobody's individual interest to safeguard and nourish it.

Ironically, as we show, even the most successful group – success being defined in terms of accumulated wealth – would have done better had cooperation and coordination been effective. So, what gets in the way? As students reflect, they discover their own deep-seated assumptions about success and how these have driven their behaviour. Peter Senge, who writes about the link between beliefs and the behaviour of systems, brings to life a number of those related assumptions in an especially rich and entertaining way that our students echo. One assumption, for example: 'Our actions won't affect the future; there will always be fish.' Another: 'You've got to win, it's that simple.' Or: 'Things are the way they are and there's nothing we can do about it'; 'If others do it, I'd be stupid not to'; 'My first responsibility is to my family'; 'Someone or something will take care of it'. And our personal favourite: 'It's just a game.' Running through the piece is what Senge describes as the Titanic Syndrome: 'If we're going down, we might as well go first class.'[3]

The Buddha's strategy advice

Here we turn to one of the first philosophers, Gautama Buddha. The Buddha was teaching in what Karl Jaspers described as the Axial Age, running from the eight to the third century BCE. The Axial Age saw an explosion of culture and thinking that influences us to the present day: it was the era of Plato, Socrates and Aristotle, and further East, the era of the Buddha and Confucius. In the Axial Age ideas travelled with traders and soldiers. Heads of the Buddha sculpted after Alexander the Great's invasion of what is now Afghanistan look uncannily like Greek representations of Apollo.

Buddhism is becoming increasingly fashionable in the West and enjoying a renaissance in India and China. But what, you might well ask, could the Buddha have to teach us about organizational strategy? After all, he abandoned his position as heir apparent to the Sakyan kingdom – a major force in the Indian sub-continent at the time – to go and sit under a tree.

The Buddha's teachings were by no means meant only for a body of monks sitting silently in seclusion. During the Buddha's extremely active life, travelling back and forth across northern India on foot, he offered guidance on how to live to a very wide cross-section of humanity. Back then (and today) his followers included people living ordinary lives as well as kings, merchants and robbers. He offered his audience a strategy.

Remember: a good strategy describes what we want to become and how we are going to get there. The Buddha's strategy was very simple. He saw that suffering is something that looms very large in life and that a fundamental human aspiration is to be free of it. He offered a diagnosis of where suffering comes from and a path towards that freedom. By suffering, the Buddha was not just referring to physical pain. He included the loss of things and people we want to have in our lives, the frustration of not getting what we want, even the sense of failing to fulfil our potential. He would have recognized suffering in Karl Marx's description of alienation and the dehumanized workplace. To banish suffering, the Buddha taught, we must get to its roots and dig them out. Suffering comes from fear, greed and delusion about who we are. By delusion, the Buddha meant that human beings tend to live as if they are separate from everyone and everything else, and that who they are is fixed.

And here – carrying our minds across 2,500 years to the present day – we see revealed the assumptions that lie behind organizational strategy as commonly practised. Seeing ourselves as separate from others, with a fixed identity, quickly leads to an 'us against the world' siege mentality, in which we interpret others' actions as 'self-interest seeking with guile', as we earlier quoted Oliver Williamson. Within that siege mentality – be it at the individual or collective level – the experience of suffering will lead us to reinforce that mentality in a vicious circle. Under siege from opportunist people around us or from larger-scale competitive forces, we will look to defend ourselves by constructing a competitive advantage.

The Buddha recommended a way of life and practices, including meditation, that would loosen the siege mentality that leads to suffering. Seeing our own lives as interdependent with others undermines the sense of us against the world. Accepting that our identities are ever changing means that change in our circumstances is not felt as an affront. We replace a narrow, contorted view of self with a much more expansive one that connects with others. A later Buddhist writer described the universe, seen through the eyes of a Buddha, through the metaphor of Indra's Net.[4] Indra was a traditional Hindu god (the Buddha, as an atheist, held that while many gods might exist in popular cosmology, like humans they could only be mortal). The Net that Indra held was an infinite web of jewels. Its distinctive feature was that in that Net you could see in each jewel the reflections of every one of them.

A philosophy of connectedness in action

Taking those insights into strategies for businesses and other organizations, the orientation is less about value capture through market dominance and more about value creation through collaboration. There are human challenges that no single organization can possibly take up on its own and which will never be addressed if beggar-my-neighbour practice prevails.

Take the Argentinean red wine that so many of us have come to enjoy over the last 15 years. The primary wine-exporting region of Argentina is Mendoza, where the vineyards nestle in the Andean foothills. Two decades ago, the quality was dreadful. Wine makers held the grape growers to ransom and the distributors squeezed value from the wine makers. Payment terms and contracts were meaningless and there was no incentive to invest in improving the vines. The truckers' union insisted that trucks could carry cargos in one direction only, to drive up freight charges. Corrupt officials demanded bribes before containers could get loaded, slowing exports to a trickle. Each producer worked on his or her own, struggling to survive. But then came what Argentinians call the Malbec Miracle. The goal was to establish Malbec – the local grape varietal – as a global brand that would benefit all those involved in the sector. The path towards realizing that ambition was collaborative. Distributors collectively agreed to a code of conduct – with scrutiny – that eliminated corrupt and predatory practices; local government saw the growers' success as key to an improved tax base; universities in Argentina and beyond contributed insight and collectively the sector funded a global marketing campaign that placed 'Malbec' ahead of any individual grower in most consumers' minds.

Many readers will know similar examples at first hand. ARM, a British technology success story, is a semiconductor company that makes no chips. It provides designs and tools for a vast ecosystem of software developers, engineers, chip fabricators and OEMs like Apple. Apple might use its bargaining power to drive down prices to gain a short-term advantage, but that does not happen, as the damage inflicted on the ecosystem would destroy the value on which Apple itself is reliant. Conversely, ARM architects have unique, trusted access to Apple's secrets to design the chip after next, and the one after that. In the ARM ecosystem – and in the Malbec region – collaboration does not drive out competition but rather creates a fruitful context for it. All are running the race with the aim of enhancing their performance as they compete with each other. By contrast, 'competitive advantage' is like seizing a head start, undermining the point of the contest.

What makes the Malbec Miracle and ARM possible? What underpins other great collaborative enterprises, like the search for the HIV vaccine, or the global financial system? The answer lies in our willingness to go beyond the us-against-the-world mentality to share our knowledge. That is not just knowledge in the form of technical blueprints, but knowledge and understanding of how others see, feel and live, calling for a deep empathy which the Buddha would have recognized as the consequence and driving force of his teaching.

> In uncertain times, empathy is at the heart of our ability to make sense of ambiguous situations, which is a critical strategic skill.

Take the Cuban Missile Crisis of October 1962, one of the most dangerous moments in human history. As air strike options were being prepared for the young John F Kennedy, the talk from the security advisers was all about 'the Soviet', and how 'the Soviet' only understood words like 'force' and 'action'. It turned out that none of the immediate security advisers had ever met a Russian. 'The Soviet' was only an abstraction, not a real flesh-and-blood human being making decisions. Fortunately for us (as the airstrikes and follow-on landings in Cuba would have unleashed a nuclear war) somebody who had met Russians entered the unfolding drama. This was Tommy Thompson, who personally knew Nikita Khrushchev, leader of the USSR at the time. He knew that war was the last thing Khrushchev sought. The Great Patriotic War – as Russians call World War Two – was only 15 years behind them and Khrushchev himself had played a frontline command role at Stalingrad: 30 million dead was enough. Thompson also knew that Khrushchev was not a dictator. Unlike Stalin, he depended on the consensus of his colleagues and could not afford to lose face. Those insights, borne of empathy, nudged humanity just far enough away from the us-against-the-world mentality to let us all live longer.

Two of us co-authors were asked to give a talk at the management conference of a major global bank soon after the financial crash of 2008. We had been asked to speak about the restoration of professional values in banking. Sadly, our talk did not go well. Just before us, the head of retail – more charismatic than any of us authors – leapt onto the stage. 'Guys!' he exclaimed (there being few women in the audience). 'Your job over the year ahead is to penetrate the customer. We must leverage the customer. I want you to take every penny you can find out of the customer's wallet and put it onto the bank's bottom line!' Our call to lofty ideals fell very flat. But rather than ideals, we should have spoken about concerns much closer to earth. In the preceding speech there were only abstractions. It was as if the speaker had never met a customer. In highly uncertain times – as they were and will continue to be – awakening empathy with the customer and her fears, hopes and frustrations is the path to value creation. Rather than speaking of an abstract entity called the customer, this is simply human-centricity, requiring the shift from the narrow self-view to the broader, more expansive view of self in the world that the Buddha recommends.

We have given you a light-hearted description of the Buddha and his teaching – asking what could be learned about strategy from someone who sat under a tree meditating all day long. We swiftly left the meditation stool to explore some of the Buddha's ethical teachings about a daily life that avoids suffering, developing a more expansive, creative, connected sense of self. But strange as it might seem, the Buddha's teachings on meditation also have a lot to offer strategists at any level. One classic meditation practice helps to develop kindness – a powerful antidote to fear and greed. The practice does not instruct us to force ourselves to feel kind. On the contrary, we are invited to recognize that at any given time there may be many different emotions within us. By giving more attention to the positive feelings we might have when we call to mind a close friend or a beautiful sunset, we can start to transform our emotional outlook, in the meditation practice itself and then in our interaction with the world. This is something that any of us might try for a few moments before we meet colleagues to discuss our organization's strategic hopes and challenges. Also, we might reflect on which elements of our strategy are driven by collective fear. How far do we really need to defend our market position against adversaries? How much margin do we really need to take from our suppliers and distributors? What are the consequences of letting our strategy be driven by unquestioned assumptions that stem from the us-against-the-world mindset? Are we missing the creative opportunities to connect with others, even at the expense of some of our bargaining power? That is not an exhortation to naïvety; the world can indeed be a dangerous place and we must at times carry the big stick. But the negative assumptions about human nature that have lain at the heart of strategy have made it more dangerous than it might need to be.

From goal to path

We began this chapter by showing how strategy, strategists and strategic leaders are centre stage in our organizations. Behind the myths and somewhat jaundiced experiences we may have of strategy, we saw its central importance to organizational life. At its simplest, strategy is about ends and means: the goal we desire and the path to get there. We took a deep dive into the goal, and how our understanding of success drives us to grasp competitive advantage which ultimately leads to the impoverishing practices of value capture, underpinned by an us-against-the-world mentality. We saw how the Buddha, 2,500 years ago, saw that mentality as the primary cause of suffering, and we heard the good news that we can reverse this mentality, opening the door to collaborative, empathetic value creation in our strategies. Ideas matter – be they the ideas of Nobel Prize-winning economists or the Buddha – because their underlying assumptions about what it is to be human will shape human behaviour. Where strategy ideas may have dehumanized our organizations, they can also lend themselves to making our workplaces more human.

So far, we have spoken only of the goal, the aspect of strategy that tries to answer the question, 'What do want to become?' But for those tasked with implementing strategy, rather than developing it – which includes the vast majority of people in any organization – the burning question is 'How do we get there?'

Those at the top of an organization typically used to say that the answer lay in a sound plan. By working backwards from a clear goal, middle managers would construct a series of steps to be taken over time. The early steps would rapidly become budget commitments and KPIs; the longer-range steps would degenerate into mission statements. The reason for this is the underlying conceit that we can both know the future and master it. That has always been a dubious claim, but in today's uncertain environment it is patently ridiculous. Rigid plans can only court escalating commitments, despite the evidence of change in the world around our organizations, and ultimate disaster.

The Buddha would tell us that we cannot predict and control events; the attempt to be the master or mistress of the universe will at best make us anxious. But we can choose how we respond to events.

In the context of our personal lives, we can respond to the adverse strokes of fortune – the loss of a job or a loved one, a neighbour dispute, failed investments – with fear and resentment. Or we can reflect on how we are responding and, without denying the reality of the matter, consider whether we can find a meaning in those events that deepens our capacity to live creatively. The same holds when fortune smiles: do we respond automatically with the popping of emotional champagne corks, or do we look to step aside from immediate reactions to explore what can be learned from our victories? In the traditional Buddhist practice of mindfulness, meditators develop the art of sensing the range of mental states – thoughts and feelings – which are left free to pass through the mind like clouds drifting across the sky. Rather than getting caught in rumination, as meditators we can learn to choose which of those clouds to let grow, in time developing the capacity to transform the contents of our minds. The traditional Buddhist view of mindfulness in this way goes far beyond the mindfulness training that HR departments increasingly offer staff to help overcome stress and feelings of alienation.

How might that serve as an analogy for the way in which we execute strategy? Just as we earlier found the dichotomy between capturing and creating value when setting the strategic goal, in strategy execution there is the contrast between the deliberate and emergent approaches. Deliberate strategy is encapsulated in the grand plan. Emergent strategy – a term first coined by management thinker Henry Mintzberg – recognizes that the plan can mislead: good strategy execution is a set of responses to the events beyond our control, that will emerge as the world changes. Rather than a linear process, emergent strategy embraces a learning loop. Taking the Buddhist meditation analogy, we would avoid leaping into immediate action by taking pains to first make sense of our situation, then make and act on choices, finally ensuring that we close the loop by finding meaning in what went wrong – and in what went right. Organizations, like individuals, that seek to flourish in an uncertain world would be wise to develop their own strategic learning loop, behind which lies the Buddha's core humanizing value of humility.

Summary

In this chapter, we focused on 'strategy' as the guide to the direction of the organizations in which we work and lead. Through the lens of philosophy, we saw how conventional approaches to strategy embed views of human nature that inevitably lead to a dehumanized workplace, and an us-against-the-world bias towards relationships. We saw that a counterforce against the gloomy underpinnings of strategy is a greater emphasis towards collaborative value creation, rather than single-minded value capture. In turn, that rests on a philosophical perspective of interdependence, famously originated by the Buddha. Alongside his philosophy, the Buddha's practical guidance on reflective meditation allows us to maintain a creative, rather than a simply reactive, mind. This serves as a powerful guiding analogy for a good strategy process in which we reflect and learn as we execute, resisting the bias towards reaction.

Questions

1 Is your organization strategy-oriented towards capturing value, or towards creating value for the stakeholders around you?

2 In what ways does your strategy open the way to collaboration with others and address the obstacles to working collaboratively?

3 Does the way in which you execute strategy incorporate a learning loop as opposed to a linear path?

Notes

1 Porter, M E (1980) *Competitive Strategy: Techniques for analyzing industries and competitors*, Free Press, New York

2 Williamson, O E (1979) Transaction-cost economics: the governance of contractual relations, *The Journal of Law & Economics*, **22** (2), pp. 233–61

3 Smith, B, Kruschwitz, N and Senge, P (2008) *The Necessary Revolution: How individuals and organizations are working together to create a sustainable world*, Nicholas Brealey Publishing

4 Fox, A (April 2013) Indra's Net metaphor cited in The practice of Huayan Buddhism, presentation to Inaugural Symposium on Chinese Buddhism, Fo Guang University, Kaohsiung, Taiwan

04

Creativity and critical thinking

'Dare to think for yourself.'

KANT

In the last chapter, we defined strategy as the dual choice of what a company aims to achieve and how it plans to achieve it. We distinguished between strategies that **create** value – by **adding** to the sum of the world's wealth and well-being – and those that merely **capture** value by simply **re-distributing** wealth amongst the competing suppliers to the same market. Creating value goes beyond the zero-sum game that characterizes so many competitive markets. As an example of value creation, we examined the global success of Malbec wine. In this case, members of the Argentinian supply chain chose to move beyond tit-for-tat competition and instead collaborate to create something of far greater value.

In this chapter we shall identify the defining characteristic of those strategies that succeed in creating superior value. We shall locate the difference in the belief systems of the various competitors. Corporate performance is a return on truth rather than on effort, alignment or intent. The creation of economic value, we shall claim, stems from knowing something that the competition does not know, particularly knowledge of competitive market response grounded in the choice behaviour of customers, employees and shareholders.

Placing ourselves in the role of an executive team, we shall argue that the task of a strategic plan is not so much to second guess the outcome of our endeavours as to surface for discussion and debate the assumptions that will determine success or failure. Performance tends **not** to rise to the aspirational level of our aims and desires; rather, it falls to the factual accuracy of our beliefs and assumptions, and therefore strategic debate should be about the veracity of our belief system rather than the achievability of our goals. The true bottom line and leading performance indicator will be the pace at which the firm is learning relative to its competitors.

The core competence of an organization is thus best expressed as the speed at which it is discovering new knowledge, based upon its skill in asking potent questions, formulating hypothetical answers, conducting decisive experiments and refining the theories in use. Treating rationality as a combination of creative and critical thinking owes much to the philosophy of Karl R Popper, and we will apply his logic of scientific discovery to the art of corporate strategy. On the basis of this analysis, we will suggest that some of the most popular concepts and practices in business serve more to hinder strategic thinking than to help it. These include notions of best practice and other formulaic recipes for success.

We begin by analysing the performance of three of the most distinguished investment managers of the last 50 years. In a capital market, as we shall explain, we can learn more about value-creating strategies than from any other market, if only because a capital market comes closest to being a pure game in which strategy is the only differentiator.

Learning from capital markets

Philosophizing about strategy is frustrated by the difficulty of isolating strategic factors as the explanation of corporate success or failure. Every market, of course, is a natural experiment in which competing ideas are being continuously tested, but the rarity of purposely structured experiments makes it difficult to know whether a highly successful firm owes its success to its strategy or to some other, non-strategic factor, such as the efficiency of its operations or the state of the economy or the play of luck. The question then is: are there any markets that approximate the conditions of a laboratory for testing strategy *per se* as the cause of corporate success?

> We have more to learn about business strategy from successful investment managers than anyone else because they are outperforming their competitors in the most efficient market of all.

We shall argue that a capital market is just such a market. First, it is a notably efficient market in which sustainable returns at levels higher than the market as a whole have been shown to be rare. If we could find an investor who had consistently beaten this most efficient of markets, then we might get closer to discovering techniques of thinking that contribute to performance and that could be imported into less efficient markets, such as customer or talent markets.

Second, stock markets come as close as markets can ever get to emulating pure games; almost all the decisions made by the players are competitive by nature and are therefore quintessentially strategic. Also, the rules of the game, and what it means to win, are unambiguous. Winners are those who achieve the highest rates of return on the capital at their disposal.

Third, the strategic moves themselves can be very simply described. They are the purchases and sales of financial instruments at discrete moments in time. The performance of a fund manager's strategy is easy to measure because it is continuously and publicly priced by the market in which it competes. This makes the link between strategy and performance much clearer and simpler to analyse than in non-capital markets.

Finally, the impact of non-strategic factors on performance is insignificant. There are no barriers to entry or exit. Scale advantages are almost non-existent. Skills of execution barely play a part. The role of operations is incidental. Qualities of leadership, teamwork, emotional intelligence, trust – and all the other interpersonal skills that influence performance in a company – play an insignificant part in the investment business. Luck has, at most, a short-term effect. To sum up, there are no factors other than strategic skill to explain differences in performance.

Therefore, when we find high levels of sustained performance in these well-informed, transparent, fair and open markets, we are witnessing something special and highly instructive – a window onto the essential attributes of strategic skill.

Peter Lynch and asymmetric knowledge

Peter Lynch managed the Fidelity Magellan Fund, perhaps the most successful, certainly the largest mutual fund of the 20th century, during its most illustrious period. Under his 13-year tenure, from 1977 to 1990, its funds under management grew from US $18 million to US $14 billion and it acquired over one million shareholders. The belief system that underpinned Lynch's investment decisions remains distinctive – and very instructive. We have quoted liberally from his autobiography, *One Up on Wall Street*,[1] one of the most revealing books ever written about investment strategy.

> Capital markets are the ideal test bed for distilling the essence of strategy.

Lynch believed fervently in first-hand, face-to-face contact with the companies – and managers – in which he invested. He would visit at least 600 companies a year. He spent almost no time in Wall Street or in the company of other fund managers. Modestly, he suggested that 'if other investors made as many calls, they too would spot the changes in corporate fortunes', which he defined as his core skill and overriding purpose. His dominant assumption was that he needed to be 'further up the intellectual food chain' than his rival fund managers.

If he had had a motto, it would have been, 'Invest **before** you investigate', a version of the ancient principle of 'Carpe Diem'. His technique was to notice the slightest opportunity in the market and to seize it quickly. He regarded the delay caused by research and analysis as fatal. The good investor cannot afford the luxury of proof; there will always be a braver soul who steals the moment.

Related to his emphasis on speed was his natural optimism. He looked for reasons to buy, not reasons not to buy. He recognized that one of the liabilities that clung to most intellectuals in the market-place was their dogged ability to construct the downside. This pessimism he always saw as the greatest vulnerability of his better-educated rivals and therefore one of the sources of his success.

He saw no advantage to be gained from discussing or setting visions, goals or targets. He knew that the aim of investment was wealth creation and that any other aim made no sense at all. He always felt that debating objectives was sterile. He found that his best results came from a sequence of surprises and that it was more effec-tive to buy without any particular long-term goal.

He brought an experimental attitude to his work, selling a stock as soon as he recognized he had made a mistake. 'You have to know when you are wrong... then you sell.' More important still, he admit-ted that most stocks he bought were a mistake.

Every winning strategy contains an element of heresy.

He enjoyed taking an unfashionable approach. Indeed, he regarded any form of orthodoxy as wholly alien to the job of a fund manager. He was a natural heretic. His only rule would seem to have been that 'to make money, you must find something that nobody else knows – or do something that others won't do because they have rigid mind-sets.'

He felt that he was in a perpetual race to the truth – hence his emphasis on speed, closeness to his sources, responsiveness and the courage to act instantaneously on his insights and intuitions. He knew that anything in the public domain – whether academic theories, news-paper stories, rumours, scientific knowledge, econometric forecasts, analysts' reports, press conferences, or public announcements – could never be the basis for his own competitive advantage. Such informa-tion would already be known to the market and priced into individual stocks. So he set himself the much more demanding role of making his own proprietary discoveries – a legal form of 'insider knowledge' based wholly on his own hard work and observational skill.

From Peter Lynch we learn that, for a decision to count as strategic, it cannot be based on the application of a universal theory or on generic notions of best practice, but on unique and situation-specific empirical insights.

Warren Buffett and market inefficiency

Let us now look at another investor, Warren Buffett. He has been described as 'certainly the most spectacular investor of modern times'. He bought control of Berkshire Hathaway as his investment vehicle in 1965, since when it has returned an average annual growth in book value of 19.0 per cent to its shareholders, compared to 9.7 per cent if invested in the S&P 500. His philosophy and style are very distinctive, and he differs in many respects from Peter Lynch. However, they both share a core set of beliefs and practices that exemplify the notion of strategy as a process of discovery. We will quote liberally from Buffett's own writings,[2] if only because he is a particularly articulate advocate of his own theories of success.

Buffett, as the archetypal capitalist, has always respected the market as an economic instrument for allocating capital productively, but he has never been in awe of it. He recognizes that it is as fallible as the human beings who continuously co-create it through their everyday judgements, decisions and transactions.

The Efficient Market Hypothesis (EMH) is the theory that, in his words, 'someone throwing darts at the stock tables could select a stock portfolio having prospects just as good as one selected by the brightest, most hard-working security analyst.' This is the theory that, since the 1970s, has become sacrosanct in the finance departments of most business schools.

Buffett acknowledges, of course, that the market is **frequently** efficient. What he believes to be a pernicious falsehood is the belief, still taught by finance professors and still accepted by many investment professionals and corporate financiers, is that the market is

always efficient. Buffett traded on this difference, citing as evidence his own arbitrage record of unleveraged returns averaging over 20 per cent per year for many decades whilst the market as a whole delivered just under 10 per cent. He is appalled that no teacher of the EMH has ever confessed to being wrong, What evidence, he wondered, would be sufficient for the advocates of the EMH to acknowledge their theory as fundamentally mistaken? 'A reluctance to recant, and thereby to demystify the priesthood, is not limited to theologians.'

The marketplace is a knowledge contest.

Buffett has spoken of the luck he felt in having competitors whose methodology was mistaken: 'What could be more advantageous in an intellectual contest – whether it be bridge, chess, or stock selection – than to have opponents who have been taught that thinking is a waste of energy?'

He has always emphasized the importance of knowing the scope and limits of one's knowledge. He limited his investments to those companies that he felt he understood. He would quote, with approval, the sentiment of Thomas J Watson, the founder of IBM: 'I'm no genius. I'm smart in spots – but I stay around those spots.'

Comparisons and contrasts between Lynch and Buffett

There are clearly some marked differences between the techniques of these two remarkable strategists:

- Lynch extolled the virtues of hard work, whereas Buffett rejoiced in his belief that 'inactivity strikes us as intelligent behaviour';
- Lynch was an opportunist, whereas Buffett was a model of self-restraint and patience;
- Lynch made thousands of small decisions every year, whilst Buffett made just a handful.

But the similarities of philosophy are far more obvious and dramatic:

- a confidence in their own, first-hand observations and in their distinctive model of successful investing;
- a determination to immunize themselves against the contagious gossip and emotions that swirl around the marketplace;
- a positive attitude to risk, expressed well by Buffett as being 'greedy when others are fearful';
- an absence of plans, targets, visions, milestones, or any other form of fixed destination;
- a distrust of publicly available information, macro-economic indicators or generic formulae as platforms for successful investment;
- a rejection of the entire academic edifice of 'modern financial theory', including the efficient market hypothesis, the capital asset pricing model, betas, dynamic hedging, and option theory;
- a recognition of the fundamental importance of experimentation as the main source of continuous learning;
- a preference for clarity over precision and for what is simple over what is obscure;
- above all, a strong heretical streak that relies upon a critical frame of mind to challenge all forms of orthodoxy, 'official' theory, and received wisdom.

Category mistakes in business

Most theories of business performance rest on the assumption that there is 'a right way' to do things. The popularity of notions such as 'excellence', 'competence' and 'best practice' testifies to the hold that this theory has on business managers. Corporate success is treated as a return on doing standard things well.

This may be true of craft skills, such as cookery, pottery and gardening, but it cannot be true of any **competitive** activity, such as sport, warfare or business. In a game of skill, there is no 'right way' of playing it. Nor can there ever be a standard way of winning.

The point of a game is that it tests a particular kind of intelligence, not the possession of a universal theory or a winning formula.

> Chess masters do not achieve their mastery through the application of 'best practice'. They are their own masters.

Any theory of business that puts forward an algorithm for commercial success is a fraud. The most it can do is to offer a suggestive method – or heuristic – either for recognizing fruitful insights or for designing conditions conducive to discovering such insights. The so-called 'scientific method' is not a method at all. It simply states the criteria for what counts as a scientific proposition (such as testability and falsifiability), and it specifies ways of testing the truth content of such propositions (such as experimentation). But the act of discovery itself remains immune from all attempts to automate it.

To believe that there can be a theory of successful strategizing is to commit a **'category mistake'**. Gilbert Ryle, a 20th-century British analytical philosopher, coined this term to identify the errors that typically arise from misclassifying an object of interest.[3] He offered the following example: a visitor to Oxford, upon viewing the colleges and libraries, asked, 'So where is the University?' The mistake made by the visitor was to presume that a University belongs to the category of **physical buildings** rather than the category of **institutions**.

Likewise, it is all too easy – and too common – to treat strategy as belonging to the category of **expert practice** (or the application of knowledge) rather than the category of **discovery** (or the search for knowledge).

George Soros and human fallibility

If we now turn from Peter Lynch and Warren Buffett to George Soros, we find a very different investor, one whose theory of investment is as philosophically subtle as it has been successful. His grasp of strategy is insightful.

The Quantum Fund, his primary investment vehicle, yielded an average annual return to shareholders of almost 35 per cent over a 26-year period – after deducting the management's participation in profits. Furthermore, Soros has a carefully constructed theory to explain his success, published as *The Alchemy of Finance*,[4] and based upon Karl Popper's philosophy of science and of the open society. All our quotations from Soros come from this text. Soros, who was Popper's student at the London School of Economics, claims that his investment record is strong corroborative evidence for the validity of his theory of financial markets, as well as being equally strong evidence against standard economic theory. No fund manager has placed greater importance upon the coherence of the philosophy underlying his investment decision process.

Like Buffett and Lynch, Soros does not believe in the theorems and methods based upon the so-called modern theory of finance and its assumption of market efficiency: 'I think that (the efficient market theory) works 99 per cent of the time, but it breaks down 1 per cent of the time. I am more concerned with that 1 per cent.' He has identified a source of systemic risk that is neglected by this theory because of its assumption of a continuous market. Soros has built a countervailing theory to anticipate the market **discontinuities** that are the real source of investment success.

Soros has said that he sees himself as an 'insecurity analyst' rather than a professional security analyst. By this he means that his sense that he may be wrong and the insecurity that this creates in his mind help to keep him alert and prepared to rectify any errors. He has always lived off his own insecurity. He could never admit to his success. His sense of his own fallibility – as well as the fallibility of others – is the source of his motivation and the foundation of his personal philosophy.

'Once we realize that imperfect understanding is the human condition, there is no shame in being wrong, only in failing to correct our mistakes.'
(George Soros)

From Karl Popper, he took the notion that critical thinking is the hallmark of science. He is always looking for defects in himself as well as in others. He pays acute attention to whether or not the actual course of events accords with his expectations. When it doesn't he realizes he is on the wrong track, and he takes great pains to discover the source of his error. He re-examines his assumptions and seeks to establish where he has gone wrong.

Owing to the main idea that animates him – that 'our understanding of the world in which we live is inherently imperfect' – Soros is sceptical of the current fad for being passionately committed to a cause or to a belief. He is wary of ideology: 'I am a thinking participant and thinking means putting yourself outside the subject you think about.' He is a strong advocate of disinterested observation.

Soros characterizes many of his competitors as workaholics who amass far more information than is necessary to reach a conclusion. He suggests that there is a danger in this approach in that you substitute data for insight: 'When you are taking risks, if you make the right judgement, if you have the right insight, then you don't need to work very hard.' Indeed, too much information can distort true judgement and too much work can detract from genuine insight. In the spirit of Buffett's admission that 'lethargy bordering on sloth remains the cornerstone of our investment style', Soros has said, 'I do the absolute minimum that is necessary to reach a decision.'

He believes that mainstream economics neglects the most important fact about economic behaviour, which he calls the principle of reflexivity. The thinking participant finds himself in the paradoxical situation of trying to predict events that are themselves shaped by those predictions. Scientists generally construe the act of understanding a phenomenon as a relationship between a passive observer and an independent reality. But when the phenomenon is an economic event, the roles of observer and participant are intimately connected. Economists make a mistake when they assume that market participants act on the basis of perfect information. There cannot be such a thing as perfect knowledge of the market for the simple reason that, as participants in the process, their thinking is ceaselessly shaping the market just as the market, in turn, is ceaselessly shaping their thinking.

Lessons of success from the capital markets

Lynch, Buffett and Soros share the following convictions:

- business success is better explained as a return on first-hand knowledge than on standard theory;
- we are inherently fallible creatures;
- dogmatic thinking is the antithesis of the critical thinking that is fundamental to strategy;
- the trial and error method of discovery – 'invest before you investigate' – emulates the mutation and selection logic of Darwinian evolution;
- sometimes we get to the truth faster by acting on the world and seeing what happens than by insisting that we think things through carefully before acting.

> Act your way into new ways of thinking.

Our claim is that these practices bear a striking resemblance to Karl Popper's description of how scientists think and work – what he called 'the logic of scientific discovery'. Popper grounded his philosophy in the practice of reason, by which he meant the exercise of our critical – *and self-critical* – faculties.

Karl Popper (1902–94) was perhaps the most influential philosopher of science of the 20th century, and remains a highly contentious figure. His dominant interests lay in the growth of scientific knowledge, the criterion for demarcating scientific from metaphysical or mythological propositions, the methodology of the social sciences and of history, and the properties of an open society.

In the following section, we will outline the central elements of Popper's philosophy of science before showing how these elements can form the essential ingredients of a philosophically coherent theory of business strategy.

Popper's logic of scientific discovery

Discarding inductive logic

Popper's main claim was that induction – the process of reasoning whereby general laws are inferred from particular facts – is a myth. Ever since Francis Bacon's pioneering attempt in the 16th century to codify the method of science, the assumption had been that the natural sciences were the inductive sciences. Scientific discoveries were the outcome of a process of data reduction. The gathering and classification of data based on impartial and repeated observation led to the formulation and justification of theories and laws. This method is, of course, still rife in the social sciences, where multivariate statistical analysis has long been the standard research method; elements of this philosophy can be found in the fashion for 'big data' and 'analytics' in business today.

There is no induction because universal theories are not deducible from singular statements. To use a famous example, the theory that 'all swans are white' can never be proved, however many swans are observed to be white, since it only takes the observation of a single black swan to falsify the theory. By contrast, refutation can be secured by a single fact. Science advances through a process of deductive falsification rather than inductive verification. In other words, the scientific temperament is one that places the emphasis on **disproof** rather than proof.

Advocating critical rationalism

Popper discarded the entire inductive edifice in favour of a deductive method, namely trial and error, or what he chose to call 'critical rationalism'.

'All life is problem solving.' (K R Popper)

Scientific reasoning begins and ends with a shared problem situation, including a mass of inherited background theories. The theories that we invent to solve our problems are conjectural ideas, wholly of our own making. They may be no more than wild guesses. Following Kant, 'Our intellect does not derive its laws from nature, but imposes its laws upon nature'.[5] By jumping to our theories rather than deriving them, we construct an imaginary world – a system of argumentative ideas formulated to explain the real world deductively. What we describe as knowledge remains entirely hypothetical for as long as it cannot be falsified. Popper describes these theories as 'nets in which we try to catch the real world'.[6]

Acknowledging fallibility

Popper challenged the conventional idea that to be rational in our behaviour is to be true to our beliefs. He denied that a belief could be rational. Indeed, he argued that rationality entailed an attitude of permanent scepticism towards our own beliefs. Rationality is intimately connected with human fallibility. By acknowledging the frailty of our belief system we become rational. In short, to be rational is to be **critical**; it is to bring all our critical faculties to bear upon anything that sets itself up as the solution to a problem that matters. Rationality pays attention to the prevailing state of science – and to the ongoing scientific debate – but it is not overawed by it.

A Popperian theory of corporate strategy, condensed into four maxims

1. Strategy is critical rationalism in action

Effective strategic thinking emulates the logic of scientific discovery. Strategy should not adhere, as is often suggested, to an inductive process for getting to ideas, starting with impartial observation, data gathering and statistical analysis, and leading to findings and conclusions. Rather, it should imitate the critical method of science, as defined by Popper:

The only intellectually important ends are: the formulation of problems; the tentative proposing of theories to solve them; and the critical discussion of the competing theories... Truth is the main regulative principle in the criticism of theories.[7]

Sterile starting points for a competitive strategy are a generic theory (for example, 'never start a price war' or 'the cost leader always wins' or 'stock markets heavily discount conglomerates') or alternatively a 'macro-picture' (for example, the future state of the economy, or the size of the potential market, or the emerging forces in the industry). Winning strategies are rarely built on knowledge that is already in the public domain. A business does not make money on the beliefs that it shares with its rivals, only on the beliefs that set it apart.

2. Strategy is a form of discovery

Albert Szent-Györgyi, a Hungarian biochemist, has suggested that 'Discovery consists of seeing what everybody has seen and thinking what nobody has thought'.[8] Every wealth-creating idea begins life as a brave conjecture. Mark Casson, an economist, has argued that:

The entrepreneur believes that he is right, while everyone else is wrong. Thus the essence of entrepreneurship is being *different* – being different because one has a different perception of the situation. It is this that makes the entrepreneur so important. Were he not present, things would have been done very differently.[9]

Strategy deals with one situation at a time. It finds its inspiration in what is unique to that situation. Strategic solutions do not generalize. They are built on insights, not rules or principles. Insights are small-scale, often short-lived discoveries. Something is noticed that had not been seen before.

Entrepreneurship, the rare skill of market making, is essentially the skill of producing just such insights and then having the courage and persistence to build them into a business. Every great business started life as the embodiment of a particularly powerful insight. Businesses decline as the discovery of new insights dries up.

3. Strategy deals in bold conjectures

Managers are not paid to make the same decisions as their competitors, however rational their thought processes. Managers are expected to carve out a distinctive approach to the future, to take the risk of being wrong, but at least to give their imagination a free rein and the chance to outperform competitors. Perversely, the more we aim to be logical in our reasoning, the harder we try to base our decisions upon established knowledge, and the closer we adhere to generic principles of strategy, the more likely we are to be driving the business towards mediocrity.

This is what makes business both frustrating and exciting and what draws intelligent people into it. Success in business rests on the intellectual courage to set aside the obvious strategy, to see through the standard solution, to go beyond the popular fad, and to steer one's own course. To be too logical is to choose to be part of the crowd. Markets do not reward herding behaviour.

Russell Ackoff, one of the founders of operational research, suggested that:

> The righter we do the wrong thing, the wronger we become. Therefore, when we correct a mistake doing the wrong thing we become wronger. It is better to do the right thing wrong than the wrong thing right.[10]

4. A strategist operates as an experimental scientist

The strategic process, to the extent that it can be formalized at all, often begins with an element of surprise and the natural curiosity that this arouses in an open mind. Surprise comes about when the predictions of a cherished theory are found to be false, or when an established practice comes up short. When this happens, the alert strategist recognizes that the market is telling him to adjust his preconceptions, however trustworthy they may have been in the past. In other words, whatever is unexpected becomes the pretext for a rational process of inquiry.

It could be said that managers draw reliable inferences from their assumptions, but that they display less discipline – and are less rational – in the attention they give to the truth of these assumptions. In other words, the errors of management are more likely to lie in false belief systems than in fallacious reasoning, hence the importance of continuous experimentation.

By way of summary, we might conclude that:

- A company's **strategy** comprises the set of problems, tentative theories, and active experiments – the argumentative structure – that encapsulates its state of play.

- To **strategize** is to have the courage to be testing a number of bold and imaginative conjectures whilst simultaneously having the humility to be searching actively for evidence that could refute them.

- For any decision to count as **strategic** it must embody a predictive theory that is proprietary to the firm, and falsifiable by experimentation.

- For a business to be run **strategically**, it must be the testbed for a continuous flow of such theories.

- To be a **strategist** is to acknowledge one's fallibility without losing confidence in one's ability to make discoveries.

- The measure of **strategic capability** is the speed at which the truth content of its belief system is increasing.

The paradox of good intentions

Examining UK government policy since the Suez fiasco, two political scientists, Anthony King and Ivor Crewe,[11] have identified a slew of 'horror stories, human errors and system failures' that they define as 'blunders' – episodes in which:

> a government adopts a specific course of action in order to achieve one or more objectives and, as a result largely or wholly of its own mistakes, either fails completely to achieve those objectives, or does achieve some or all of them but at a totally disproportionate cost, or else does achieve

some or all of them but contrives at the same time to cause a significant amount of 'collateral damage' in the form of unintended or undesired consequences.

These are some of the blunders that they identify and elucidate:

- Acts of government, such as the 1971 Industrial Relations Act, the 1975 Community Land Act, the 1991 Dangerous Dogs Act, the 1995 Child Support Act, the 2003 Licensing Act.
- Initiatives, such as workers' cooperatives, care in the community, the poll tax, railway privatization, super-casinos, housing information packs (HIPs), anti-social behaviour orders (ASBOs), ID cards, private finance initiatives (PFIs), the Millennium Commission, individual learning accounts, tax credits and debits, the Assets Recovery Agency, and the Rural Payments Agency.
- One-off decisions such as the investments in the Blue Streak missile, the Concorde aircraft and the DeLorean car, the exit from the ERM in 1992, the raid on pension funds in 1997, and the abolition of the 10p starting rate of income tax in 2007.

In most of these cases, so King and Crewe argue, the remedy has exacerbated the problem. When it does so, and as our best efforts prove to be self-defeating, we become more and more puzzled, disenchanted and demoralized.

If we turn from government mistakes to corporate incompetence, we find no shortage of practices that bear comparison with any of the blunders identified by King and Crewe. Many business practices resemble nothing so much as a form of displacement activity. Instead of focusing on the design of better solutions to pressing problems facing their customers, managers devote their time to bureaucratic rituals such as the mission statement, the balanced scorecard, the triple bottom line, the corporate risk register, the social responsibility audit, the stakeholder charter – initiatives that have the appearance of being professional and progressive, whilst absorbing huge amounts of managerial time in counterproductive activity. Gary Hamel, a strategy professor, has priced 'wasteful bureaucracy' in the American economy at over three trillion dollars a year, or 17 per cent of US gross national product.[12]

When Tim Ambler, a marketing scholar, researched the behaviour of the executive boards of UK companies, he discovered that, 'on average, boards devote nine times more attention to spending and counting cash flow than to wondering where it comes from and how it could be increased'.[13] And in the same vein, Rory Sutherland, President of the Institute of Practitioners in Advertising, offers this explanation for the sluggishness of the UK economy (or indeed those of most other Western economies) when he points out that:

> Anyone exposed to current business publications would be forced to conclude that the best means of creating business value and growth lies in mergers, balance-sheet manipulation, takeovers, outsourcing, off-shoring, downsizing, tax avoidance, restructuring, leverage... anything, in other words, that does not involve the tedious business of finding out what people might want and then providing it profitably over time within a relationship of deepening trust.[14]

Managerial incompetence, whether in business or in government, is camouflaged as 'state of the art', 'leading edge' or 'best practice', portentous phrases that attempt to conceal the emptiness at the heart of the activity. Harry Frankfurt, a Princeton philosopher, posed the question, 'Why is there so much bullshit?'[15] It's a good question, to which part of the answer is that we're easily duped into believing that any policy that comes either loaded with good intentions or dressed up in the vernacular of managerialism will deliver good outcomes. In effect, bullshit expands whenever the requirement to make sense exceeds the possession of knowledge.

The moral to be drawn from King and Crewe is that we **overestimate** the importance (and the piety) of our visions, missions, aims, measures, and plans as guides to action... just as we **underestimate** the importance (and the truth) of the assumptions that underpin the actions we take in pursuit of these goals. We naively believe that what separates effective from ineffective policy is righteousness of purpose rather than solidity of evidence, and that good people with good intentions get to good results, and vice versa. Indeed, this is how we typically assess a policy or a strategy. Was it motivated by virtuous intent? In other words, we judge the quality of a strategy by the quality of the strategist. As a result, we are easily seduced by a flawed strategy if it compellingly proclaims its own virtue.

An open mind

If we truly believed that many of our assumptions are mistaken, then we would approach decision making in an entirely different frame of mind. We would not justify our beliefs by seeking corroborative evidence; we would look instead for disconfirming evidence. The confidence we bring to a decision should not rely upon a wealth of supportive data but the difficulty of finding any strongly disconfirming evidence.

In arguing with others of a different persuasion, we would take more interest in the path that **they** had taken to **their** beliefs than in defending the process by which **we** had reached **ours**. We would want to strengthen those points of view that **differed** from our own before attempting to challenge or refute them. We would make the assumption that the likelihood that they had alighted on the truth was no less – or no more – than our own. Our only concern would be for the truth, irrespective of authorship. Indeed, in the dialogue that leads to a shared point of view, we would forget which idea had originated with whom.

At the dispatch box, or in *Newsnight* interviews, or in pre-election debates, the typical mood of antagonistic argument – all too often a dialogue of the deaf – would, just occasionally, be punctured by a question or an observation arising out of pure, disarming curiosity: 'How interesting…', 'What brought you to this view…?', 'Perhaps you have a point…', 'I hadn't thought of it that way…', 'What an intriguing suggestion…', 'How might we build on your idea…?', 'Why on earth hadn't I thought of that…?', 'Help me develop my own understanding…'.

Rationality belongs to the disinterested mind, one that is not trying to prove something, or win an argument, or sway a crowd. It is a mind that is open to innovative ideas, to alternative viewpoints, to new data... as well as to the discomfort of being disconcerted.

Conclusion

Rationality in business can be interpreted in at least three quite different ways:

1 A rational action is one that **identifies the best means to a given end**; it is grounded in the widespread belief that a successful business is one that achieves its goals. This is an assumption that unites and drives the majority of executives, and the operational practices most closely associated with this belief are management by objective (MBO) and strategic market planning.

2 A rational action is one that **flows logically from existing knowledge**; it is based upon the idea that a well-made business decision is the application of evidence-based theory. This is an assumption that is most closely associated with the academic world of business schools and departments of economics, as well as management consultancies; it is exemplified in the use of the case study method and in the application of managerial concepts such as best practice, total quality management and operational excellence.

3 A rational action is one that is **taken with the intent of discovering new knowledge**; it originates in the formulation of a question to which a good answer would endow the firm with a competitive advantage. This is the assumption that underpins scientific discovery and motivates most entrepreneurs, and it finds its best expression in design thinking and continuous experimentation.

Strategic thinking should unashamedly be wedded to the third of these definitions, the one that, in effect, defines rationality as the 'art of the soluble', to borrow Peter Medawar's definition of the scientific method.[16] It assumes that a firm's performance is ultimately determined by its pace of learning relative to that of its competitors. Thus, rationality in business is construed as a process of experimentation whereby managers act on the world to create the data from which they derive their theories. Winners know something that losers do not.

Questions

1 Are the strategic plans of your business essentially the numerical objectives you want to achieve, the best practices you want to adopt, or the belief system you want to test?

2 What is the question to which a good answer would contribute most to the performance of your business?

3 What candidate hypothesis would you most want to test as just such an answer?

4 How could you design an experiment to quickly and cheaply test this hypothesis?

If strategy is a series of experiments, the question we ask in the next chapter is, 'What is the role of the leader?'

Notes

1 Lynch, P (2000) *One Up on Wall Street*, Simon & Schuster, First Fireside edition, New York

2 Buffett, W (1997) *The Essays of Warren Buffett: Lessons for Corporate America,* selected, arranged and introduced by Lawrence A. Cunningham, Carolina Academic Press

3 Ryle, G (1949) *The Concept of Mind*, Hutchinson, London

4 Soros, G (2003) *The Alchemy of Finance*, John Wiley, Hoboken, New Jersey

5 Ibid, Section 12

6 Ibid, Section 12

7 Ibid, Section 7

8 Quoted in Good, I G (1962) *The Scientist Speculates*, Heinemann, London

9 Casson, M (1982) *The Entrepreneur: An economic theory*, Barnes and Noble, Totowa, New Jersey, p. 14

10 Quoted in Caulkin, S (2006) The more we manage, the worse we make things, *The Observer*, 1 October

11 King, A and Crewe, I (2014) *The Blunders of Our Governments,* Oneworld Publications, London

12 Hame, G and Zanini, M (2017) Assessment: Do you know how bureaucratic your organization is? *Harvard Business Review*, 16 May

13 Ambler, T (2003) *Marketing and the Bottom Line,* Pearson, London

14 Sutherland, R (2009) Why advertising needs behavioural economics, *Campaign,* 23 October

15 Frankfurt, H (2005) *On Bullshit,* Princeton University Press

16 Medawar, P B (1967) *The Art of the Soluble*, Methuen, London

05

A question of example and fairness

In this chapter, we challenge the prevalent view that leadership is primarily about providing direction, laying down the rules and ensuring that others stay focused on achieving the organization's goals. We offer an alternative, a person who leads by example and sees fairness as the foundation for performance. If we are to avoid the alienation that so many people feel at all levels in the organization and focus our leadership energy and influence on creating an environment in which we and others can flourish, we need to think and act differently. We need to ask the question, how can the organization serve people, not only our customers, or our shareholders, but the people who give their time and energy to each other and to the work we are doing together? We need to work on the example we set in our behaviour and put ourselves in others' shoes, to see things from the perspective of others. We must challenge whether we are working together on the basis of fairness. With the help of 20th-century philosopher John Rawls we see that fairness is not a simple question of handing things out equally. It involves taking responsibility for our contribution; it requires an acknowledgment of difference; it requires constant vigilance from all parties. It is the work of leadership. With the help of the ancient Greek philosopher Plutarch, we explore what it is to be an exemplar, a person that others want to emulate, a person whose presence builds confidence and inspires us to be at our best.

A world divided

Most theories of leadership make the tacit assumption that the world is divided into those who lead and those who are led, implying that it is somehow right and natural that the former should be free to exercise their own agency to a much greater degree than the latter. Likewise, hierarchical relationships, reporting structures, control mechanisms, sign-off procedures, financial incentives, planning systems, commitment processes – indeed, the entire apparatus of a modern-day bureaucracy – serve to undermine the sense that who I am and what I do counts, our innate sense of personhood that lies at the heart of a human and moral community.

Let us start with the story of an extraordinary 20th-century leader who had no need of hierarchy, bureaucracy or managerialism to lead a phenomenally successful organization.

Max Perutz and the Cavendish Laboratory

In 1936, a young and penniless Viennese chemist, Max Perutz, from a Jewish family, fled Austria and arrived in Cambridge to study for a PhD. After the war, he was to become the 'godfather of molecular biology', the recipient of a Nobel Prize for the discovery of the molecular structure of haemoglobin, and the founder of the most successful biological research laboratory in the world.

In 1947, with the help of Sir Lawrence Bragg, Perutz won support from the Medical Research Council to set up the MRC Unit of Research for the Molecular Structure of Biological Systems at the Cavendish Laboratory in Cambridge. The only other staff member was John Kendrew, Perutz's first PhD student, who would share his Nobel Prize 15 years later, by which time the unit had grown to 90 researchers and had become the Laboratory of Molecular Biology (LMB). It was the home of, amongst others, Francis Crick and James Watson, the discoverers of the molecular structure of DNA.

Perutz was the chairman of the LMB from 1962 to 1979, its most illustrious period. By the time of his death in 2002, its legacy as a single laboratory had been to produce nine Nobel Prizes (shared amongst 13 scientists), four Orders of Merit and nine Copley Medals (the highest honour awarded by the Royal Society).

How did Perutz achieve so much? What was his secret?

First of all, he kept the administration of the lab to a bare minimum. This is how he described the culture he sought to create:

> Creativity in science, as in the arts, cannot be organised. It arises
> spontaneously from individual talent. Well-run laboratories can
> foster it, but hierarchical organisation, inflexible bureaucratic rules,
> and mountains of futile paperwork can kill it. Discoveries cannot be
> planned; they pop up, like Puck, in unexpected places.[1]

Revealingly, he wrote: 'I rarely plan my research; it plans me.'

Sir James Black, the pharmacologist, reflecting on the manner by which Perutz inspired his people and nurtured their research, described it thus: 'No politics, no committees, no reports, no referees, no interviews – just highly motivated people picked by a few men of good judgement.'[2] César Milstein, one of Perutz's most distinguished research students, spoke of what he learned most from Perutz: 'I learned what research was all about... I always received an unspoken message which in my imagination I translated as, "Do good experiments, and don't worry about the rest".'[3]

As a result, the lab became a prodigious magnet for the brightest young scientists. All those who worked with Perutz remarked on his gentleness, his tolerance and his appreciation of others. One of his co-researchers described him as 'a humane scientist who used his brilliance to illuminate and not to dazzle others'. Kiyoshi Nagai, a Cambridge colleague, said this of him:

> (He) taught his students and post-docs to be independent and rarely
> asked how things were going. However, he was often working next
> to us and was always ready to listen. When he travelled to the States,
> he talked to people about my project and always brought back some
> ideas. For two years I had nothing good to tell him, but he was always
> supportive.[4]

Perutz fostered independence of mind in his young scholars. He led by example, spending more than 90 per cent of his time working at the bench, and expecting others to do likewise. He kept up to date with the work of his colleagues by hooking up with them over lunch or coffee in the canteen that his wife, Gisela, had designed to act as the intellectual hub of the laboratory. Everyone was treated with the utmost respect, humanity and affection. He was once heard to say, with his typical modesty, that his only responsibility towards his talented flock was to ensure that they got whatever they required to keep going.

> To lead you must know not the technical answers, but what the people you depend on need, what they are passionate about.

Leading in a spirit of fairness

What can we learn from Max Perutz? What is special or seductive about the way he led the lab?

First, he shows that an organization can be highly effective with a very **light touch**. The lightness comes from Perutz's ability to exercise power through influence and inquiry rather than through authority or seniority. He placed himself **alongside** his colleagues as one scientist amongst many.

His power resided in his **character**. Those who found themselves in Perutz's presence and open to his influence would have ascribed their changing attitudes and behaviour not to his brilliance but rather to their own skill and effort. They will have **internalized** the process. This is the irony of leadership. For Perutz, this would have been a source of pleasure. He neither needed nor sought to take credit for the influence he had.

The style of leadership that Perutz exemplified flatters us into becoming better people than we otherwise would be. It draws out our higher capabilities, particularly our creativity and courage, and it weans us off our weaker nature, such as our compliance and fatalism. We live up to the trust that is placed in us and the expectations that are placed on us. We are reminded of our best self – the person we want to see when we look in the mirror.

It is what we notice as **missing** in the Cavendish Laboratory that sets it apart – what we are surrounded by in our organizational life that drives us mad, but that we have come to accept as just how it is, at the same time moaning about it to anyone who will listen. In the Cavendish Laboratory there was no need to moan; there were no targets, benchmarks, plans, key performance indicators, time clocks, and the like.

Just a few years ago, General Electric, the organization credited with introducing KPIs (key performance indicators) – to drive people to ever-increasing heights of performance – gave up and rid their organization of such counterproductive nonsense. KPIs do not drive performance; they drive connivance. If you want your call centres to maximize their call response, do not expect your business to maximize its customer loyalty. The quickest way to get rid of a call is to transfer it, not to resolve it!

Perutz's operating assumption was that those with whom he worked were just as trustworthy, ambitious, honest, and diligent as he was himself. Why would anyone employ someone who is aimless, feckless and thoughtless? Perutz would have regarded it as a source of shame to feel that he had to rely upon the use of hierarchical power or bureaucratic compliance to bring out the best in others. By dispensing with control, with management, he was purposefully placing the emphasis on the individual scientist to perform according to his own or her own passion and ambition. He was treating people as individuals with their own personal agency.

The lab was successful not because attention was focused on its performance, but because everything revolved around the individual and the conditions that were most conducive to their practice – their specialism and natural desire to develop mastery of their subject. Perutz did not perceive his colleagues as human resources. They were **persons**, who would surely flourish if treated as persons. Everything began and ended with the individual, scientists at the bench doing their own work, either individually or in small self-selecting teams. Perutz was alongside them, doing his own work – but taking a particular interest in theirs.

Plutarch's exemplum

'Example is not the main thing in influencing others; *it is the only thing.*' This sentiment goes to the heart of anyone's success as a leader. Leaders know instinctively that power is used most wisely and beneficently when it has no need to draw on the authority vested in it. They focus instead on setting a good example.

In 1984, Casper was sentenced to 30 years in a US jail for violent crimes. Sixteen years later he was released, not because he was innocent, but because he chose to become a positive role model. After years of working his way up the criminal hierarchy to become the most feared prisoner within the prison community, in his own words, he had an epiphany. He realized he was acting out a story, a vision of himself that he had not chosen. Yes he had made choices, bad choices for which he was responsible, but he made those choices in the context of a story about himself that he had never questioned, until now. The narrative he had adopted without question was not uncommon. Coming from a family with an abusive father, a drug dealer, who eventually left, surrounded by gangs and having to protect himself against attack, he became violent and angry. At the moment of his epiphany Casper decided to take control of his own story, to decide what he wanted to be for himself. To do so meant challenging the expectations of his peer group and members of his family. Today Casper travels the world providing a role model to people – young people, old people, white people, black people – in organizations and in communities, helping them to transform their self-image to a positive image and dare to dream again.

Human beings are intensely social animals whose behaviour is strongly shaped, whether consciously or not, by their fellow creatures. **We become whom we spend time with**, continuously perceiving others as models to emulate and standards to measure ourselves against. In the classical world, this technique was known as the exemplum, or the moral example. Contagion need not be unconscious and passive. We can actively construct our moral environment. Casper is an exemplum.

Well aware of this, the ancients deliberately used the **exemplum** to steer people in good directions. The most famous practitioner of this technique was Plutarch, the Greek philosopher, priest and historian of the 1st century AD. A born teacher, he cared passionately about how to instil character in young people, and for many centuries his method was at the heart of Western education. Indeed, for many centuries he was regarded as 'Europe's schoolmaster'.

Plutarch believed that each person was a combination of reason, emotion and habits and that, with encouragement, most of us can become sufficiently self-willed to change our habits through the use of reason. We can select our role models. We can bring to mind great figures either from real life or from literature and history and resolve to live up to their standards. He argued that 'character is habit long-continued'.

The mimetic theory of character was clearly influenced by Aristotle's idea that each of us acts our way into the person that we become. Thus, if a particular virtue to which we aspire is not coming naturally to us, we need not fret about how to acquire it. Faced by a situation that calls for courage, for example, we imagine what a courageous person would do in this situation – and then do exactly that. We pretend to be someone we are not. And gradually, over time, we become that person.

With this in mind, Plutarch composed his great work, *Lives of Grecian and Roman Noblemen*, more commonly known as *Parallel Lives*. Here he tells the inspirational life stories of 46 of the most eminent military and political heroes of his time, including Alexander the Great, Cicero, Brutus, Pericles, and Pompey. He wanted his readers not merely to hear about their deeds but to set their heart on living up to their example and steering their own course by them:

> Our intellectual vision must be applied to such objects as, by their very charm, invite it onward to its own proper good. Such objects are to be found in virtuous deeds; these implant in those who search them out a great and zealous eagerness which leads to imitation.[5]

Different ages and ideologies alight upon different kinds of exemplum. They construct their own myths and write their own fables. Thus while the early Christians found Plutarch's choice of heroes perverse, they nevertheless remained convinced that heroes served a noble purpose. So they invented the saint. In Renaissance Italy, Giorgio Vasari's *Lives of the Great Painters* offered a heroic vision of the artist, while Machiavelli drew upon the 'actions of illustrious men' to educate the prince. During the 19th century, writers such as Goethe, Carlyle and Nietzsche created a different ideal again, that of the romantic hero.

Organizational behaviour and procedural fairness

To flourish at work is to be treated fairly by our co-workers, particularly by those who are more senior than us. Perhaps fairness should be regarded as the first virtue of a well-led organization, and leadership as the skill of creating just such an organization.

> A sense of fairness in the workplace is the pre-condition for being at our most human and behaving in a way that is good for us and for others.

But what do we mean by fair? As with trust, we intuitively know what it means. We recognize its presence – *and particularly its absence*. But how can we clarify the concept to the point where we can apply it practically – as leaders ourselves – so as to inject greater fairness into the organization for which we work?

In *A Theory of Justice*, John Rawls invented a famous theoretical device for analysing the problem that he called a 'veil of ignorance'.[6] The idea is simple. Instead of the rules being set by those in authority, 'those who engage in social cooperation choose together, in one joint act, the principles which are to assign basic rights and duties and to determine the division of social benefits.' The veil of ignorance applies because until the negotiations are over, no one knows their role, their position, their duties, or their rights and therefore must ask the question, if they were assigned any of the roles would they consider the associated duties and benefits fair? 'The principles of justice are chosen behind **a veil of ignorance.**'

What are the principles that we should expect to emerge from such a debate? What did Rawls himself believe to be the rules of distributive justice? How did he envisage the discussion proceeding?

Rawls argued that, behind a veil of ignorance, we would choose two general principles of justice:

1 **the principle of equal liberty**: each person has an equal right to the most extensive liberties compatible with similar liberties for all;

2 **the difference principle (or the maximin rule)**: social and economic inequalities are justified only in so far as they benefit the least advantaged persons – and if they attach to positions that are open to all under conditions of equality of opportunity.

For Rawls, society should be perfectly free to engage in collective activities, such as commerce and trade, that lead to some people having more power, income, and status than others, provided that these activities simultaneously make life better for all. In other words, advantages accrue to everyone as a consequence of a certain degree of inequality.

In developing his theory of 'justice as fairness', Rawls was particularly concerned with what people would regard as a just distribution of **wealth**, but his thought experiment applies equally well to the question of a just distribution of **power**. Rawls alludes to the application of his theory to 'private associations' such as companies, as well as to society as a whole, but he never pursued this line of inquiry. We suggest that Rawls' model of justice has direct application to the world of business and to the design of the workplace, and that, behind a Rawlsian veil of ignorance, very few people would design the organizational forms in which they find themselves living and working today.

The language and practice of both leadership and management – at least in their normal, everyday form – typically offend against principles of fairness and equity. All managerial theories, from Frederick Winslow Taylor onwards, rest on the premise that the organization is the end in the service of which its employees are the means. Thus, economists treat labour as a 'factor of production' like capital or land or equipment; accountants measure 'human capital' as a cost to be optimized; and corporations treat employees as 'human resources' to be put to work as management sees fit. In the vernacular, we speak of employees as 'working for the company'; far less often do we hear the company described as 'working for the employee'.

> We are missing the point in the way we talk about strategic goals and organizational values. It is not the organization that we serve, it is each other, people. The foundation stone of service is fairness. Anything else is instrumentalism using position power to gain personal advantage.

When, in his prophetic book *Images of Organization*, Gareth Morgan characterized some corporations as 'psychic prisons',[7] he was observing how far short so many firms fall from the ideal of the good organization. Yet in Max Perutz's LMB we get a tantalizing glimpse of how close it is possible to get to a place where each individual's purpose and passion is embraced and how much more rewarding, in every sense, such an organization would be.

Fairness in practice

A just society is a society that if you knew everything about it, you'd be willing to enter it in a random place.

JOHN RAWLS, *A THEORY OF JUSTICE*

Rawls has laid the foundations for an elegant alternative organizational model for how power gets distributed, how decisions get made, and how gains get shared – in short, for how the inequalities inherent in any collective endeavour get handled. It remains an intriguing question as to how, in today's world, the employees of a typical company would define fairness if engaged in the veil of ignorance exercise. Would they, for example, argue for a flatter, more democratic organization? How much inequality would they be prepared to countenance? Would millennials come to different conclusions from their older, more experienced colleagues? Would they, for example, be less risk averse and more meritocratic in the distribution of rewards? Would the executive board regard the entire process as misconceived or even mischievous? These are **empirical** questions.

How feasible is a debate of this kind amongst the members of a real organization? Would it be possible to 'bring to life' Rawls' thought experiment? Could we imagine our way into the original position, stripped of any knowledge of our own achievements, talents, resources or opinions? Could we enter authentically into such a debate without any of the (self-serving) biases that we had acquired with our experience of life? Could we de-personalize ourselves sufficiently to come to a genuinely disinterested and impartial view of what would constitute 'fairness at work' and a just social contract for the enterprise to which we belong?

As an exercise in organizational renewal, we suggest you conduct the following experiment:

1 pick a random sample of employees;

2 bring them together in a room for a day;

3 invite them to enter into a Rawlsian debate;

4 notice the conclusions to which such a 'self-less' discussion would lead.

In seeking to find a blueprint for fairness, there could hardly be a more important organizational practice than conducting these kinds of conversations across the enterprise. In doing so, however, **prepare to be surprised**. It is not self-evident that a broad cross-section of staff would dismantle the entire apparatus of leadership and management. People might be more discerning, more careful, and more conservative. It could be surprising how much hierarchy and bureaucracy most people would regard as 'fair and beneficial' – particularly in moments of crisis, or in those cases where experience and expertise are called for. But also, be prepared for shocks. Much of what we take for granted at work could equally as well be strongly challenged.

Our own experience is that the majority of people at work would prefer a greater sense of inclusion, a more active role in the choice of goals and the design of strategies, particularly those decisions that most affect them, and much greater discretion in how they do their job and discharge their responsibilities. We have practised such experiments both as consultants and when in general management positions. In short, we have found that people wish for a greater sense of identity, belonging and purpose at work whilst also acknowledging their obligation, in partnership with their colleagues, to co-create the organizational environment that would play to these desires.

Here are examples of four celebrated companies that play to a very different set of rules from the norm, rules that are explicitly designed to create a greater sense of inclusion and fairness.

Morning Star and the colleague letter of understanding (CLOU)

A CLOU describes things like the colleague's purpose within the organization and the activities that the colleague agrees to accomplish. Each year, every employee renegotiates their CLOU with the colleagues who are most affected by their work. This is the system by which the employees of Morning Star, the world's largest tomato processor, reach agreement with each other as to who should expect what from whom. CLOUs are voluntary contracts, mainly across the internal value chain. The commitments they make are not hierarchical. They are to those whose success depends crucially upon the quality of their service to them. Fairness, in this case, is allowing employees to forge their own mutual agreements.

CLOUs are just one of the practices that contribute to Morning Star's democratization of its business. Others of their radical practices include the following: no one reports to a boss; instead, every employee is expected to negotiate their responsibilities with their peers, particularly those whose own work is most dependent on the fulfilment of these responsibilities. Thus, compensation decisions are grounded in peer-based assessment; indeed, all signs of hierarchy and rank, such as titles, organization charts, or promotions, are shunned. Everyone is expected to equip themselves with the tools they need to meet their negotiated responsibilities, being trusted to spend the company's money to do so.

Morning Star was founded in 1970 and is headquartered in Woodland, California. It employs 400 people and turns over US $700 million a year.

WL Gore and the lattice organization

'We vote with our feet. If you call a meeting, and people show up, you're a leader.' This is how WL Gore, the US $2.5 billion high-tech materials company, discovers its leaders. They are not appointed; they emerge through a democratic process. The teams that form around them are self-selecting and self-managing; even the choice of their CEO is a group decision.

For 50 years, WL Gore has demonstrated, if ever it needed proof, that there are alternative ways of running a highly successful company than adopting traditional managerial practices. The Gore culture operates on the radical assumption that great ideas can originate at any level of the organization, that all ideas, whatever their provenance, should compete for funds on an equal footing, that the firm's resources are best distributed not by being **allocated** from above but by being **attracted** to the best ideas from below.

Thus, the Gore model resembles a marketplace of self-defining and self-organizing groups more than a hierarchy of pre-ordained positions and pre-specified tasks. As with any market, it places as much emphasis on competition as on cooperation, it puts its faith in meritocratic principles, it mercilessly exposes mediocrity, it relies upon intrinsic motivation more than financial incentives, and it values a person's contribution more than their credentials. The role of leaders in WL Gore is to facilitate this process rather than direct it or orchestrate it. Fairness is here defined as self-management.

HCL and reporting to the customer, not the boss

> We must destroy the concept of the CEO. The notion of the 'visionary', the 'captain of the ship', is bankrupt. We are telling the employee, 'You are more important than your manager'. Value gets created between the employee and the customer, and management's job is to enable innovation at that interface. To do this, we must kill command-and-control.

These are the words of Vineet Nayar, from 2007 to 2013 the CEO of HCL Technologies, a US \$5.5 billion global information technology services company based in India, and now Founder and Chairman of the Sampark Foundation.[8] Turning the organization through 90 degrees, such that it faces outwards to customers and not upwards to managers, was his main mission whilst at HCL. For him, fairness would have been equivalent to interpersonal and inter-departmental trust.

Nissan and fair process dialogue

Recovery, creating new sustainable growth, is one of the toughest challenges facing a well-established business when it runs into financial difficulties. Yet Nissan's turnaround between 1999 and 2001 is a celebrated example of how, using the right method, it can be achieved with panache. In this case, the method was 'fair process', a version of procedural justice advocated by W Chan Kim and Renée Mauborgne,[9] both of them professors at INSEAD.

For a decision to be perceived to be fair, they argued, those responsible for implementing it should feel that their viewpoint was solicited, understood and respected, that the debate was open and objective, and that the rationale for the ensuing decision was clear and disinterested, even if their own ideas were rejected. They used a three-fold model – *the 3E model* – for testing the fairness of their corporate culture:

- **Engagement**: those affected by any corporate decision are involved in making the decision; for example, their ideas and arguments are solicited and their right to challenge the ideas and assumptions of other parties is honoured.

- **Explanation**: those engaged in this process fully understand the rationale by which the ultimate decision is made; in other words, they appreciate the impartiality of the process, whatever the outcome.

- **Expectation**: those implicated in executing the decision know clearly in advance the criteria against which they will be assessed.

Fairness lies in the perception by everyone involved that the playing field is level.

> What lessons can we take from these four examples? The hope is that, however difficult a Rawlsian discussion might be and however arduous the journey towards a set of consensual conclusions, it would nevertheless serve to move an organization to one imbued with the virtues of fairness and distributive justice.

A dangerous collusion

Too often we outsource responsibility for our lives to others in the naïve belief that they will manage us better than we can manage ourselves. We deceive ourselves into believing that they have our interests and welfare at heart. We want to be looked after – and so we place our faith in those who have arrogated to themselves a 'duty of care' towards others such as us. We call them 'leaders', and place our faith in their ability to understand our interests better than we do ourselves. We want leaders to release us from the responsibility, indeed the obligation, of living our own lives according to the light of our own reason and volition.

As leaders we can so easily be seduced into responding to such needs by providing the answers, laying out the rules, making the decisions, rewarding and penalizing as we see fit. In this way, we can justify our seniority and greater pay. As leaders we enjoy the control; as the led we enjoy the lack of responsibility.

This collusion is contagious. Numbers of managers and levels of management continue to grow. During the 20th century, Britain increased the size of its managerial class *sevenfold*. In today's Chinese army, one-third are officers and another third are non-commissioned officers. Soon there will be an insufficient number of subordinates to keep these bosses and leaders occupied. Why would a firm want to employ someone who needed managing? Why would a self-respecting leader want to lead someone who needed leading? Why would anyone want to take responsibility for someone who was unwilling to take responsibility for themselves?

In the next four chapters, we set about challenging this state of affairs. With the help of other philosopher friends, we reframe what it means to lead, what it means to co-create, what it means to learn and transform, and what it means to take responsibility. To be an exemplar. We dig deeper into three of the major preoccupations of organizational life: empowerment, communication and engagement.

Questions

1 Would you describe your workplace as 'fair'? In other words, would it pass the 'Rawls test'?

2 If not, which particular aspects of interpersonal behaviour or institutional design fall short of the principles of a just organization?

3 Would others in the firm describe you as an exemplar of leadership, and which of your qualities do they regard as particularly exemplary?

Notes

1 Perutz, M (2003) *I Wish I'd Made You Angry Earlier: Essays in science, scientists, and humanity,* Cold Springs Harbour Laboratory Press

2 Quoted by Andrew Tucker in his Obituary of Max Perutz, *The Guardian*, 7 February 2002

3 Ibid

4 Quoted by Kiyoshi Nagai in his obituary of Max Perutz, *The Biochemist*, June 2002

5 Plutarch, *Parallel Lives* (SMK Books, 2014), translated by Aubrey Stewart

6 Rawls, J (1971) *A Theory of Justice*, Harvard University Press, Boston MA

7 Morgan, G (2006) *Images of Organization*, Sage, London

8 Quoted in Hamel, G (2012) *What Matters Now,* Jossey-Bass, San Francisco, p. 234

9 Kim, W C and Mauborgne, R (2003) Fair process: managing in the knowledge economy, *Harvard Business Review*, January

06

The gift of authority

Introduction

In this chapter, with the help of the 17th-century philosopher Thomas Hobbes and the 18th-century philosopher Immanuel Kant, both of whom were to square the circle of individual needs with collective responsibility – the drive for personal fulfilment with the need for community – we present an approach to authority that can help all of us to square that circle. The approach recognizes that authority is not a right but a gift bestowed by others and is to be used for the benefit of others. Central to this is the idea of empowerment. We look at how the typical attitude to empowerment, taken by even the most well-intentioned leaders, is fundamentally flawed. We explore what it means to use the authority gifted to us to create an environment in which empowered people can flourish.

Tell them we feel un-empowered!

A few months ago, we were invited to give a keynote speech and run a workshop at a diversity and inclusion day for a client in Europe. The session was well attended by middle managers and staff. Everyone participated enthusiastically, and at the end of the workshop several participants spoke to us. Their message was clear and simple: 'You have to tell senior management that we feel completely excluded and *un-empowered*, boxed in by rules and regulations with no *authority* or *freedom* to make decisions.'

As it happened, we were scheduled to report back to the management board that same evening on how the session had gone. We dutifully reported the message: 'Your people feel un-empowered and excluded.' The response from the senior executives on the management board was sincere and alarmed. Recovering from their surprise and being conscientious and responsible people, they turned their attention to generating ideas to fix the problem. 'We will organize breakfast meetings, where anyone can come and tell us whatever they want to'; 'let's start a staff suggestion scheme'; 'we should invite a staff representative to join part of our management board meetings'; 'we will initiate an empowerment training programme'.

Problem sorted?

This response to the accusation of a lack of empowerment is not uncommon. The question we ask in this chapter is: will the responses of our well-meaning senior executives actually lead to empowerment? In our experience they do not.

The Cambridge dictionary defines empowerment as the process of gaining freedom and power to do what you want, or to control what happens to you. The important word here is *gaining*. Unfortunately, the way in which those *with* authority have come to think of empowerment is that it is their job to grant empowerment to others. Equally unfortunate is the way in which those *without* authority have come to think of empowerment as something that needs to be given to them. This leads not to empowerment but to dependency. This is the path of least resistance and is a collusion that allows those seeking empowerment to avoid taking responsibility and allows those being asked to grant empowerment to maintain their control.

We need to focus on the word *gaining*, rather than *granting*, in our thinking about empowerment. We need to develop leadership practices to help people exercise their freedom and deploy their power. This is the focus of this chapter. How do we use what authority we have to best serve empowered people?

What can philosophy tell us about how to use our authority to support empowered people?

In answering this question, we focus on the thinking of our two philosophers, Thomas Hobbes (1588–1679) and Immanuel Kant (1724–1804). Through Hobbes we will challenge the notion that authority is delegated downwards. In any situation other than a dictatorship it is in fact delegated upwards by the consent of others, with the duty to use it for the benefit of others. Through Kant we will explain what it means to exercise the authority we have for the benefit of others. So much of our management practice is instrumental, seeing others as a means to an end; Kant refocuses us on seeing others and behaving towards them as an end in themselves.

It is a tribute to the quality of their insights into the human psyche that an Englishman from the 17th century and a German from the 18th century have so much to offer us in our modern 21st-century, thrusting world of business, with multiple KPIs, bonuses to strive for, colleagues to compete with and foreign holidays to organize. The basic needs of people for meaning and self-expression have changed little if at all in the last 3,000 years. And the questions of how power is distributed between people and what is legitimate authority are as relevant to us today as they have ever been.

The best of intentions

Let's get back to our senior executives who were wrestling with solutions for their 'un-empowered' staff. We left the story at the point where the senior executives had suggested a number of initiatives to solve the problem and bring about an outbreak of empowerment.

All the ideas they came up with seem on the face of it helpful and empowering. But if we take them one by one, we see an underlying premise that runs counter to their intent to empower. Take suggestion schemes. If I have to make a suggestion to someone more senior than me in order to get something done, then by definition I am not empowered to do it – I need permission to do it. If I need to be invited to a special breakfast meeting in order to tell people more senior than me what I think, I am by definition not empowered to tell them what I think, unless invited to a breakfast meeting to do so. If I need to be represented to make a case to someone else to make a decision, I am by definition not empowered to make the decision. And if I consent to being sent on an empowerment training programme, I am already in denial that empowerment is a state of mind and not a skill set that can be trained. I am colluding.

> The premise that undermines each of these empowerment initiatives – suggestion schemes, representation, breakfast meetings, training – is that power lies with the hierarchy and empowerment is the act of someone more senior in the hierarchy simply taking account of, or at least considering, the input of someone more junior in the hierarchy before making their decision. This is not the enactment of empowerment; it is the granting of permission and the reinforcing of dependency.

We get it upside down

Let's turn each idea on its head for a minute and see what comes out.

How about a scheme entitled: 'Just do what you think needs to be done – tell me you have done it, or tell me you are thinking of doing it, and if I need to input I will let you know.' Not very catchy we agree. But, if put into practice, as a way of enabling people to get on with what they think is the best thing to do, it would definitely support an empowered way of behaving. Even in highly regulated sectors there is great scope for increasing the space for empowered people to act with fewer constraints. One of our clients, a global pharmaceutical client, is experimenting with removing the entire budgeting control paraphernalia and simply asking the country manager to aim high and report on performance.

How about hiring people who consider it their duty to tell others, more senior or in different departments to them, what they think others need to know to help them do their job even better? And with respect to people already hired, how about making it clear that it is expected that people tell others what they think they need to know? Forceful contributions are required from everyone. This is what is valuable – people who contribute with conviction.

Several years ago, we were working with a major insurance company that launched a fantastically successful product. Sales soared and the applications processing department was overwhelmed. The organization hired temporary staff to cope with the demand. This meant that less experienced staff were processing applications; mistakes increased and the time it took to process applications lengthened. The trade press started reporting on the fiasco and sales began to decline. Early one Saturday morning, the head of the applications factory, knee-deep in applications, rang the CEO, **interrupting her breakfast**, and simply said, 'You need to get down here now!' Not a typical command to your CEO, but essential. The CEO dutifully appeared and was horrified at what she saw. Application forms stacked high on makeshift tables, phones ringing unanswered and supervisors tearing their hair out trying to answer the deluge of questions from the novice staff on what to do next. Monday morning, she brought all the functions in the product value chain together: the sales departments, the media department, the complaints department and the applications department. By the end of the day they had worked out a plan to rescue the situation and put the product on a firm and sustainable footing. This was only possible through the empowered behaviour of the head of the applications factory and the CEO deciding to use her authority to create an environment in which empowered people could collaborate to solve the problem.

What if leaders, like our CEO above, saw themselves not as superiors but as representatives of other managers and staff, ready to facilitate and intervene to remove barriers? What if, instead of occupying themselves in executive meetings in which they deliberate on how to direct affairs, they took up positions on the shop floor in order to see and feel how the organizational infrastructure for which they are responsible – the rules, the allocation of resources, the physical conditions – gets in the way of people trying to do their best work? These are the things that leaders have the *authority* and responsibility to change. What if they used their authority to remove and reduce the barriers? What if they created an environment in which empowered people could flourish? This is how Max Perutz, who we met in Chapter 5, chose to lead.

We want to emphasize the critical shift in thinking that we are advocating. Conventional thinking about empowerment is that people need to be given permission to be empowered. You hear all the time senior executives extolling their people to 'take more risks', 'be more innovative', 'do what is right for the customer'. It does not work; people do not need to be told these things – to be given permission. Gary Hamel, Professor of Strategy and Entrepreneurship at the London Business School, often points out that in their private lives, people are all these things – creative, risk takers, doing what they believe in. We are instinctively creative, we are passionate about what we care about, we seek out new experiences – holidays, cuisine, activities – taking risk. The job of leadership is to create an environment in which creative, passionate, curious, risk-taking people can flourish, develop themselves, make a positive difference and infect others with their enthusiasm.

> If we turn traditional ideas on their head, then those higher up in the hierarchy don't gift empowerment to others, rather they create the space in which empowered people can flourish.

Authority is a gift

To understand and explore the idea that the job of leaders is to create an environment in which others can flourish, we need to see seniority not as a privileged position from which gifts can be discretionally bestowed on others, but as a gift from others with associated duties. To do this, and to make the required shift in management practice, we need to challenge how we think about authority in organizations.

Organizational authority stems from the role someone has in the organization. We often talk about delegated authority, where maximum authority resides at the top of the hierarchy and the least authority lies at the bottom. Many organizations use delegated authority matrices, stipulating which authorities have been delegated downwards, in hierarchical terms, and to whom, to make sure everyone is clear on who can make what decisions. We believe that the idea that authority is delegated downwards, once again, is upside down.

A classic example of downwards-delegated authority is spending rights – the amount of money a person can spend without seeking authority from a higher level in the hierarchy. Typically, the CEO has the authority to spend a large amount of money and can delegate authority downwards to lower levels of the hierarchy to spend smaller amounts. Those lower down can in turn further delegate spending rights for increasingly smaller amounts to others even lower down the hierarchy. Eventually, you get to a level where a person cannot spend a penny. There are reports from some organizations where individuals literally have to ask permission (which is sometimes denied) before they can 'spend a penny'.

The assumption behind this top-down view of delegating authority with ever decreasing degrees of freedom at each lower level in the hierarchy, is that more senior people are more qualified to make more costly, impactful, or weighty decisions than less senior people. The idiocy of this approach becomes very quickly apparent if you consider hospitals. Paramedics looking after patients being rushed to hospital in the back of an ambulance sometimes have to make life-saving decisions. Paramedics are not the most senior people in the hierarchy of the medical profession. While in many organizations, the decisions that people need to make at lower levels of the organization may not involve life or death, they often have the potential for creating much more customer value than the decisions made in the CEO's office.

Coming back to our example of spending rights, the question of who should have the most spending authority should not be answered on the basis of seniority but on the basis of how well positioned a person is to make good decisions on behalf of the organization and its goals. And by positioned, we do not mean a person's position in the hierarchy or level of education, we mean their knowledge, their experience, their understanding of the context and their ability to act to make a positive difference.

The problem with all attempts to coordinate and control what happens in an organization through clearly defined lines of authority, supported by delegated authority matrices, is that it is impossible to do so. We are told there are only two certainties in life: taxes and death. But there is a third: if you can't adapt you become redundant. The corporate graveyard is full of once-great companies that failed to adapt in the mistaken belief that if they just kept following the process, procedures and conventions that had become cemented into their core they would survive. We have to move away from thinking in terms of legislating, controlling and planning.

> The world in which we live is complex and has so many disruptions, threats and opportunities, unforeseen circumstances and novel experiences that there is no one set of delegated authorities that can legislate for all permutations. Worse still, by thinking you can legislate in this way and expecting everyone to behave accordingly, you simply make your organization less adaptable and fit for the uncertain world we live in. Adaptability is not achieved by controlling what happens; it is achieved by invention in the face of what is happening. The point is not to make people responsible but to allow people to be response-able.

Over the last two years we have conducted research with over 100 organizations from across the world on the behaviours that facilitate flourishing and adaptability. The findings are unambiguous. Directive, hierarchical and controlling behaviours undermine the ability of others to flourish. Curious, experimenting and inquiring behaviours create the space for others to flourish.

The most common approach to tackling the rigidity and lack of adaptability stemming from the classic delegated authority approach has been to consider different models of authority. This has led to much debate about alternative organizational and cultural models, whether to be a hierarchy, a matrix, a meritocracy or a holacracy. The problem is that the subsequent responses from those in charge, to implement structural and process changes, are much like rearranging the deck chairs on the Titanic. Whatever organizational and cultural model we seek to establish, we cannot escape the fundamental questions that each of us has to answer for ourselves: **What is right? What authority do I have? By what right do I have it? Who am I serving with it? How should I use it for good?** These are philosophical questions, not economic, psychological, structural or process questions.

A question of philosophy

The practice of authority, imposition of rules and creation of laws has been a central concern of philosophers and theologians for millennia. The concern is, to what extent and in what form do we need to exercise authority to enable beneficial, productive and respectful cooperation between people in a society or community? The solutions that have been promoted or adopted, whether religious, democratic, dictatorial or philosophical, all recognize some form of authority superior to the authority that each of us has over ourselves, our right to privacy, to decide what is best for ourselves and to 'own' assets that we have rightfully acquired.

For any superior authority to be willingly accepted by people who are free, created equal and with the power to govern themselves, it must be thought of as 'just', that is considered to be morally right and fair within the values of the community. What is considered morally right and fair is not a matter of science, it is a matter of philosophy. In the next sections, we'll explain how the ideas of Hobbes and Kant have shaped our understanding of what is, and what we accept as, the just, morally right and fair exercise of authority. We share our view of how to use the power we have, based on our authority, justly on behalf of others. Of course, any person may use authority unjustly (at least if they have superior force on their side) but that would not constitute the proper use of authority. If people use power outside the remit of authority it is simply a form of bullying dressed up as authority.

> Authority is not a right associated with position, it is a gift bestowed by others to be used on the behalf of others. If executed without the 'permission' of others, it is not authority, it is the unjust exercise of power – bullying.

Thomas Hobbes – we are born equal

Thomas Hobbes, an English philosopher (1588–1679), is credited with creating the foundation of what is generally accepted as the social contract basis for liberal democracy. The social contract is an agreement between the members of a society, organization or community, in which certain individuals are given specific authority. The authority they are given is to be used to coordinate the productive collaboration of the members of the society or community, or, as Hobbes called it, the commonwealth. This too is the function of organizations and the role of leaders within them.

Hobbes lived in a period dominated by the struggle between royal authority and parliamentary authority in England. The English civil war between 1642 and 1651 saw a battle for supremacy between the Kings, Charles I and Charles II, and Parliament. The result was effectively the beginning of the inexorable shift of power from regal rule to parliamentary rule in England.

It was in his best-known book *Leviathan*,[1] that Hobbes established his social contract philosophy. At the heart of this philosophy was the idea that all men are born equal with the power to govern their own lives. Despite this somewhat radical thinking, given he was writing in the mid-17th century, Hobbes, like most of us, was also a product of his time. During the civil war he was a supporter of regal rather than parliamentary supremacy and exiled himself to France from 1640 to 1651, where he was a tutor to the Prince of Wales, later to be Charles II, who was also exiled in France.

While making the case that all men are created equal, he was an advocate of regal rule to adjudicate between the power struggles of men, who did not seem, in his view – and with considerable evidence to back him up – to be able to settle their differences among themselves without recourse to violence. An individual's right to power over their own life too often spilled over into the use of power to limit the lives of others. Those with more power, such as the command of greater resources, set about securing a better life than those with less power or limited command of resources. Hobbes termed this unrestrained power struggle 'a war of all against all'. In Hobbes' mind, to engage in a war of all against all was effectively to commit suicide – a sin against God.

Hobbes saw that the only way out of this power struggle, which led to much violence and human suffering, was for all people to accept his view that legitimate power (authority) must be representative, based on the consent of others. This is a view that many people did accept and still accept today. This did not lead him to conclude that democracy is the best form of legitimate authority over others. Instead, he settled on the view that there must be a ruler who rules by right. In his mind, only a superior authority, a sovereign, could be accepted and allowed to overpower, where necessary and in specific aspects of life, the self-governance power of each individual. Given the context of centuries of rule by monarchy, this is not such a strange conclusion as it may seem today.

While we may be less inclined than Hobbes to depend on the benign inclinations of an all-powerful ruler, we have a lot to thank him for. Hobbes gave great credence and considerable momentum to the idea that we are created equal with power over ourselves. The compelling resonance of this idea is so strong that not only was Hobbes' thinking an inspiration to the Founding Fathers in constructing the US constitution, it is more or less universally accepted as true for most people in the world today. As leaders it is our duty to act accordingly. A leader is a leader if others follow through choice, because of the example set, or the vision shared, or the confidence instilled, or the protection provided.... The people over whom we have authority may comply through force but only follow by choice. Empowered people do not stay if all they get is orders to comply. We all know the truism: people leave bosses, not organizations. Equally, people follow bosses to new organizations.

> An organization populated by the compliant is an organization where leadership is conspicuous by its absence. An organization populated by followers is an organization where leadership is evidenced through its abundance.

Hobbes' insights into the relationship between power, authority and community provide a strong foundation for the idea of just leadership:

1 we are created equal;

2 the authority we have is lent to us;

3 the power that stems from our authority is to be used justly in the service of others;

4 if poorly used it can be taken away.

Simple and hard to disagree with, although Hobbes would not have gone quite as far as to include the fourth statement. His view was that once a commonwealth has been established, 'they that are subjects to a monarch cannot without his leave cast off monarchy and return to the confusion of a disunited multitude'. Nonetheless, many monarchs throughout history have found to their cost that if they lose their backers they can come to a sticky end. So in reality, point 4 applies even to monarchs.

> Do you examine your behaviour, your intentions, your decisions and actions in the light of what it means to be a just leader – do you?

We see the principles of the social contract at the heart of many of the contracts that frame our cooperation within and between organizations today – employment contracts, partnership agreements, supplier contracts, etc. Such contracts attempt to limit the arbitrary exercise of power and oblige us in turn to comply with certain duties. But contracts alone do not determine behaviour, create great leadership or enable empowered people to flourish.

Immanuel Kant – we are duty bound

A contract is a form of authority, and like all authority can be enacted for good or bad. We must turn to others to build on Hobbes and unshackle our fortunes from the whims of an all-powerful sovereign, a bad boss, a selfish colleague or the exploitation of a 'contract'.

To do this, we turn to the German philosopher Immanuel Kant to seek a source of legitimate authority, not based on a sovereign, a metaphysical being or their representative on earth. For Kant, legitimate authority stems from what it means to be a person, seeking to cooperate and settle disputes peaceably and productively in society – able to delegate our power to self-govern in certain respects for the greater good.

Kant was born almost 150 years after Hobbes in a period of unprecedented social, religious and political change. The certainties that stemmed from centuries of village and community life, such as knowing your place in society and knowing it was unlikely to change in your lifetime, were under threat.

As early as the 1750s, an emerging middle class, with aspirational expectations of improvements in quality of life and education, were challenging accepted wisdom and established authority. The widespread availability of printed material fed the appetite for new ideas. The number of books published in Germany jumped from 78,000 in the first half of the 18th century to 116,000 in the second half, a 50 per cent increase. The number of new titles published per capita in Germany was one of the highest in Europe, second only to Great Britain, a country already well on the way to constitutional monarchy. No longer was it a given that the sovereign authorities, emperors, kings and queens, ordained by God, could expect to have their power unquestioned.

Kant's contribution to what constitutes a just exercise of authority stems from his formulation of the categorical imperative in his work, *Groundwork for the Metaphysics of Morals*.[2]

The categorical imperative comprises a number of formulations – expressions of what it means – three of which are particularly instructive for us as we look at the nature and just use of authority. The formulations in their original form are somewhat impenetrable, but we give details of the three we are concerned with below. In essence they state that:

1 You should use those principles to guide your actions that you would insist on all others using to guide their behaviour – this is the universalizability formulation.

2 You should not treat others as a mere means to an end but also as an end in their own right – this is the humanity formulation.

3 If we are to cooperate in society we should act as if we were following the rules of a society in which everyone was treated as an end in him/herself – this is the Kingdom of Ends formulation.

It is common that in our organizational world we think about people as human resources, and in economic terms as factors of production, and habitually treat each other as a means to an end. This contrasts with the way, outside of organizational life, we place people at the centre of our societies as citizens that the government must serve to help us to live healthy, fulfilling lives – at least that is the general idea of democracy and the mantra of the benign dictatorship.

Kant's focus on treating human beings as an end in their own right was highlighted recently during a strategy workshop with the board of a European bank. We were facilitating a workshop when the discussion turned to the role of culture in successful strategy execution. At this stage the finance director expressed her concern that people were being treated as a means to an end and suggested that the Human Resources Department should be renamed the People Department. Whether or not the renaming of the department would have the desired effect is another matter, but what this conversation demonstrates is the growing recognition and concern in organizations that the way we think of people is at odds with what it means to be a person. Two weeks later in a workshop with senior executives from a global bank, a question from the chief executive was being debated: how do we humanize our organization?

Returning to Kant and his categorical imperative, we see that he was committed to finding a universal maxim that could be used as the basis for the ethical conduct between people, to enable each and every one of us to flourish and to cooperate with others. This is an ambition that organizations and society at large should share.

It is important to recognize that Kant was keen to demonstrate that behaving in a just manner is a rational activity, that is, an activity that any thinking sentient being would conclude is the right thing to do. He believed that all people are equal, have autonomous wills and possess the faculty to subject themselves to the laws they create in order to live together in a state of cooperative and communal living. Does this remind you of Hobbes? Kant adds that this 'autonomous will' governs our actions in such a way that we are not simply victims of our selfish desires and impulses; we are able to act in accordance with a sense of what is right or what is our duty. To be rational and act based on reason rather than driven by emotions or selfish desires. Kant argued that it is the duty of the reasoned person to educate others to be able to live the reasoned life. Even Adam Smith,[3] the founding father of capitalism, a model based on the 'invisible hand' of self-interest as the basis for wealth creation, believed that, for the greater good, we are all inclined to over-ride our self-interest: 'How comes it that our active principles should often be so generous and so noble?'

Kant's theory of the autonomous will is related to Hobbes' insistence that all men are created equal and with power over themselves. The key additional point that Kant insists on is that in exercising our power we have an innate sense of what is right (an ability to reason) that overrules our immediate desires.

The categorical imperative and leadership

So, what do Kant's formulations of the categorical imperative mean for business, organizations and leadership? To recap:

1 The formulation of universalizability stipulates that is our duty not to behave in ways to others that we would not want them to behave to us, and to behave to others in ways that we would want them to behave to us.[4]

2 The formulation of humanity stipulates that it is our duty to treat others as ends in themselves, not simply as a means to our ends. We must consider others as people in their own right with legitimate goals of their own that they are seeking to realize. In our interactions with them we should not let our needs of them, to support our goals, dictate the way we treat them. Rather our respect for others' ends should dictate the way we treat them.

3 The formulation of the Kingdom of Ends stipulates that it is our duty to be subject to the laws we make. We are both sovereign, in that we create the laws, and subject, in that we obey the laws we create, as will others. This is the consequence of the two formulations above: as we make laws on the principles of universality and treating people as ends in their own right, the laws we make apply equally to ourselves as to others.

4 In summary, these formulations of Kant's categorical imperative give three transformational guidelines for leadership:

   a. behave towards others in ways that we would want them to behave towards us;

   b. our respect for others' ends should dictate the way we treat them;

   c. the laws we make should apply equally to ourselves as to others.

In Kant's Kingdom of Ends, which he devised as a thought experiment to explore the implications of the categorical imperative, we are by definition all both sovereign and subject. Sovereign in that we make the laws by which we should live, and subject in that we are bound to live by them. In effect we delegate our authority over ourselves in certain just respects to the Kingdom to which we belong. We do this by delegating specific authorities to defined offices of the state, and by association the persons occupying the office.

We could argue that this still does not imply an acceptance by any of us of others having authority over us. But in practice we do; this is what always happens in real kingdoms – as opposed to Kant's hypothetical thought experiment – in organizations, in businesses, in communities, in empires, in countries.

> We appoint and recognize individuals to play roles with authority over the rest of us. But the important point is that the acceptance is based on the authority being exercised justly. If it is not exercised justly, it is an imposition and is resented, and at the first opportunity it is taken away.

In a civilized society, and equally in a business or organization staffed by empowered people, those that have authority over us are those we have, by agreement, delegated authority to, for example the police, judges, politicians or the boss, the finance director, the supervisor, audit team.... They in turn are responsible for creating a society, business or organization in which those of us that abide by the laws we create and subscribe to can flourish.

While in organizational life it may at first appear that we have no choice in our boss and cannot remove them, or withdraw the authority delegated to them, in practice we can. There are many ways in a modern organization in which an unethical or incompetent boss can be stripped of their authority or have their excesses curbed. Unconsciously bad bosses can be helped to become consciously better bosses using tools such as 360 feedback. Corporate governance is designed to ensure that business is conducted within a legal and ethical system. Employment tribunals function to protect individual employees from abuses. Collective action is a means of securing a more equitable distribution of resources. These mechanisms have evolved to ensure that the recipients of upwards-delegated authority work to use their authority for the benefit of others.

> Authority is not delegated down the hierarchy, it is delegated up the hierarchy. Those of us lucky enough to reach leadership positions would do well to reflect on this.

Of course, none of these mechanisms work without those subject to the authority standing up when required to call out excesses, incompetence or misdemeanours. We will explore further what this means in Chapter 10.

The chief ethical officer (CEO)

In our organizations, it sometimes seems that we have taken a step back in time to a feudal world in which people exercise power through a sense of right and entitlement rather than duty and service. We believe that authority is a gift and a responsibility. A fundamental job of leadership is to create and safeguard an environment in which others can flourish. The CEO, other c-suite members, and leaders in general, should think of themselves not so much as the chief executive officer but more as the chief ethical officer.

Earlier in the chapter we discussed the spending rights at each level in a hierarchy. In our alternative organization, the chief ethical officer would be concerned with ensuring that the money is available to be spent according to the decisions and insights of the people with the knowledge and responsibility for achieving an agreed outcome. The chief executive officer, under the pressure of constant demand for improved performance, can easily become more concerned with ensuring no money is spent without authorization – especially if it may dent the profit margin promised to the investors upon which the CEO's success is being assessed.

There are of course many chief ethical officers and leaders at all levels in organizations that act ethically and create flourishing environments. Nonetheless, we are confident that all of us can seek to do better. Here is an example of just such a person acting as chief ethical officer.

CASE STUDY

Nestlé Philippines

In 2003, Nestlé Philippines Inc. (NPI) was a $2 billion-turnover profitable business riding high on the Asian consumer boom, one of Nestlé's top 10 markets worldwide. By 2004, the company was seeing a flattening of sales growth, a shift in discretionary consumer spend to mobile telephony, and increasing competitive pressure across product categories. Q1 2005 saw a drop in sales of 17 per cent, a severe build-up of pipeline stocks, ageing stocks on shelves, unhappy distributors (holding excess products), several overflow warehouses, and 600 containers waiting to be unloaded at the port, with penalty charges of millions of dollars.

Most of the company was unaware there was a crisis. The sales team was busy on an incentive trip they had earned by loading pipeline stocks in 2003. There was no sharing of information. The organization worked as if each department was a completely separated silo, unconnected, with each function sitting on a different floor, in enclosed wooden partitioned stalls and with frequent finger pointing.

Nandu Nandkishore arrived in 2005 as the new CEO of NPI. Nandu set about a turnaround by focusing everyone on the strategic choices that needed to be made and what businesses NPI could win in. Instead of providing the answers and telling people what to do he asked questions of those who do the work – the marketers, the sales team, the procurement team: what are the cumbersome processes that are tying up cost? What could we do differently to plan sales, stocks and manufacture, product by product, according to demand? How do we get control of working capital? In so doing, he made it clear that all present were **response-able**; he believed they were the ones best placed to work out what to do. Importantly, he created a physical and behavioural environment in which empowered people would flourish. He gave them the time, the space and the respect to get on and work it out together. He saw his role as removing the barriers to collaboration and contribution. The wooden partitions came down. Functions were brought together in product teams to break down silos. Nandu role-modelled team behaviour and collaboration. The old behaviours of finger pointing and silo-based performance were replaced by joint ownership and co-creation. Nandu's principles were simple and Kantian:

- The power I have is vested in my role which has been given to me – it is a gift. My job is to use it to enable others to flourish as I have been given the opportunity to flourish (**behave towards others in ways that we would want them to behave towards us**).

- The people who work here are capable, have a contribution to make and want to do a good job (**our respect for the ends of others should dictate the manner in which we treat them**).

- What I expect from others, I will demonstrate through behaving as I would want others to behave (**the laws we make apply equally to ourselves as to others**).

NPI turned around in 18 months, and thereafter achieved milestone after milestone, becoming at the end of five years one of the best-performing Nestlé operations globally, with sales growth, profitability, market share growth, employee satisfaction, zero working capital, and outstanding marketing and communications.

Key ideas

- *Empowerment is not the discretional granting of permission.* The premise that undermines most organizational attempts at empowerment is that power lies with the hierarchy and empowerment is the act of someone more senior in the hierarchy taking account of the input of someone more junior in the hierarchy, before making their decision. That is not empowerment; it is simply the discretional granting of permission.

- *The job of leadership is to create the space for others to flourish.* By turning conventional thinking on its head we see that the role of those higher up the hierarchy is not to gift empowerment to others at their discretion, but to create the space in which empowered people can flourish.

- *Legislating for all possibilities makes your organization less adaptable.* The complexity and disruption of the uncertain world in which we live creates so many threats and opportunities, unforeseen circumstances and novel experiences that there is no set of delegated authorities that can legislate for all permutations. Worse still, by thinking we can legislate in this way and expecting everyone to behave accordingly, we simply make our organizations less adaptable.

- *Authority is not a right associated with position.* Authority is a gift bestowed by others and to be used on the behalf of others. If executed without the 'permission' of others, it is not authority, it is the unjust exercise of power – bullying.
- *Upwards delegation.* Authority is not delegated down the hierarchy, it is delegated up the hierarchy. Those of us that reach senior positions would do well to reflect on this.
- *Let others decide.* Instead of focusing on including the views of managers and staff in their decision making, leaders should focus on creating an environment in which empowered people can make the decisions needed to succeed.
- *The power that comes from authority is to be used justly.* It is our duty to exercise what authority we have, justly.

If you want to make better use of whatever power and authority you have:

- act on the belief that we are all created equal;
- remember the authority we have is given to us;
- behave towards others in ways that you would want them to behave towards you;
- understand and respect the ends (goals) of others and use that understanding to dictate how you treat them;
- apply the laws you make for others equally to yourself.

Conclusion

We have explored the relationship between empowerment, authority and power. To be a better leader, think and act differently and use your authority to create an environment in which empowered people can flourish. Ask yourself the following questions and endeavour to keep them at the front of your mind and at the top of your priorities:

- How can I deepen my understanding of what matters to others and use that understanding to connect people and create opportunities for them?

- What can I do to make it easier for others to do their job and shape their jobs in ways that play to their strengths and enthusiasms?

- What do I need to do to remove impediments to the natural curiosity, creativity and craft of those around me?

In the next chapter we explore how, in creating an environment in which others can flourish, our approach to communication gets in the way and needs to change. The idea that the higher up the hierarchy you are, the more you know, and that your job is to make sure others understand and act on what you know, flies in the face of how we learn, make sense and commit to action.

Notes

1 Hobbes, T, *Leviathan* (1651)
2 Kant, I, *Groundwork for the Metaphysics of Morals* (1785)
3 Smith, A, *Moral Sentiments* (1759)
4 Kant does make a distinction between perfect duties such as not murdering, which is our duty all the time, and imperfect duties that one does as much as one can, such as being charitable.

07

Meaning and communication

We have just seen in the previous chapter how we need to turn our thinking about empowerment on its head and focus on creating an environment where empowered people can flourish. One critical ingredient in this is our approach to communication. People need space to create their own meaning. Yet too often we see well-intentioned leaders, in pursuit of providing clarity, simply telling people what to think and why.

With help from three philosophers, Epictetus (55–135 AD), David Hume (1711–76) and Jonathan Haidt (b. 1963) we explore how the 'tell' approach to communication inadvertently undermines something at the very core of human nature – our need to make our own sense. We will see the damage that is done when we fail to appreciate how humans seek to make sense of their context and make meaning for themselves. We will unravel the issues and challenges to see that the job of leadership is not to tell people what to think or how to act, through the art of brilliant communication, but to create a space for them to make their own sense and meaning, from which coordinated action will follow. All too frequently our client conversations begin with stories of resistance, lack of buy-in, or people failing to step up. In our experience none of these labels represent what is going on. The problem is the leaders' approach to communication.

The great cascade

We gather as instructed for the quarterly 'all company' Town Hall meeting. The CEO, backed by a specially commissioned video and a fully branded set of PowerPoint slides, announces the new strategic focus and operating model. Various boxes and arrows depict the 'as-is' and 'to-be' structuring of business units. Finally, the new strap line, 'Beyond the Horizon: innovating for a better future' adorns the screen. The CEO reminds everyone that for the organization to be more innovative, the culture, among other things, needs to change. 'Beyond the Horizon' is about everyone striving to reach new frontiers.

In the 15-minute Q&A that follows, shortened to five minutes because the CEO overruns, he answers two questions before apologizing for the lack of time and inviting everyone to keep the questions coming by using the 'Ask_the_CEO' mailbox that has been created specifically for the purpose. The CEO concludes by instructing all managers to *cascade* the key updates that will be circulated to management grades and feed back any questions that may arise to the central communications team. Finally, he reassures all that any rumours about restructuring meaning redundancies are false. In the following months, managers will be reinforcing the 'why' and the 'what' through cascade communication, ensuring everyone is 'bought in' to the new operating model. Volunteer change agents will be appointed to support each business unit – applications are now open! Formal proceedings having been successfully completed, everyone troops off to the launch party carrying their freebie pens and canvas bags emblazed with 'Beyond the Horizon'.

Does this sound familiar? With slight variations this remains the dominant approach to developing understanding to drive collective action: the carefully orchestrated Town Hall meeting, the managerial cascade of curated information, and a (hopefully) persuasive change agent network.

Let's get to the heart of the matter – within each of these distinct activities, if we look closely, we can identify an implicit prescription of what to think, how to feel (and often) what to do. We call this the 'tell' approach. Whilst not always overt, the tell approach is at the heart of the majority of coordinated efforts to drive action in organizations. Those more senior have already determined what needs to happen; the focus is on everyone else understanding it, agreeing with it and acting on it. But what is the impact of such an approach? The leadership team are up late (again) rehearsing the content for the Town Hall, feeling pressure to have all the answers. Everyone else is left overwhelmed and confused about what it all means for them. Of course, it is only natural for any of us trying to create change for the better to strive to build understanding of the change we want to bring about and to secure long-term sustained commitment to action, these are understandably the preoccupations of leaders today. But as we will see, this go-to approach to communication only destroys creativity, diversity and commitment to action.

Why is telling so compelling?

First, let's explore why this approach is so prevalent throughout the world. Some research we conducted into how senior leaders approach executing strategy sheds light on the issue. We were interested in what leaders turned to most as their go-to activities when executing strategy. We found that 89 per cent of them did one of three things below:

1 alter organizational structures – who reports to whom;
2 change who is accountable for what and who can make related decisions;
3 introduce new processes to make things run smoothly.

This was the story across the world, irrespective of industry. It is not surprising, given we all have a need for certainty and closure. It is human nature to prefer working with the tangible, things we can specify and monitor, and when something is not tangible, we will do our best to make it so. When we know what to do and can easily see and measure our progress, we feel in control and this makes us feel good.

The second part of our research explored a different and potentially more important question – what were the barriers to making things happen? What got in the way of strategy becoming action? Once again we saw a consensus, irrespective of industry and culture: it was the lack of human interaction.

The fact that we intuitively know what the biggest barrier is – a lack of human interaction – yet still choose to focus on changing structure, process and who makes decisions, is an interesting phenomenon. We have come to call this the *Tyranny of the Tangible*.

The tyranny of the tangible and the fallacy of control

As we began to explore with leaders this knowing-doing gap, we hit upon the crux of the issue. Leaders were worried that if they weren't seen to 'take' control they would 'lose' control and they felt the best way of maintaining control was to execute more efficiently changes to one of the three things – structure, process and accountability for decisions. The irresistible pull of the tangible is driven by our innate desire to feel in control with respect to our responsibilities. This makes sense; most of us want to feel we have done a good job. The mistake, of course, is acting as if we have more control than we do over the outcomes.

The consequences of the control response to activities and communication can be observed in most organizations. The symptoms include anxiety, passivity and dependence – often recognized by leadership simply as 'resistance'. But these are natural reactions and they tell us very little, if anything, about people's commitment and engagement with change. Anxiety reduces our propensity for exploration, creativity, collaboration and external focus. Our perspective shrinks, we become attuned to threats and personal risk looms larger. Leaders complain that morale is low. People appear resistant and obstructive; they ask lots of questions or perhaps none at all. The truth is we all feel insecure when we have not had a chance to make sense of things and to do so in relation with others whom we trust.

Change initiatives are typically time critical, another reason why we are so often attracted to the speed and immediacy of the tell approach. At the very time when leaders most need their carefully crafted words translated into action, they find the opposite happens. Despite desperately wanting and encouraging everyone to 'take the initiative', 'step up' and not 'wait to be told', they find the opposite happens: people become passive, they create expectations that the leaders have all the answers, and when adequate detail is not forthcoming, or messages are open to interpretation (as they always are), confusion sets in. This phenomenon is a consequence of the *transmit-receive* construct at the heart of the tell approach. The transmit-receive nature of cascade communication creates a consume (as opposed to create) reaction. Although the words being expressed may urge people to be proactive and innovative, the method – the broadcast tell – reinforces a response of 'wait for further instructions'. The dissonance that results leads to inaction and dependence as people await further information and clarity.

How we act will always trump **what** we say. Try this small experiment next time you are with a large group of people. Ask everyone to bring their outstretched hand to touch their **cheek** and at the same time to watch you carefully. As you say this, take your own outstretched hand and touch your **chin**. Ninety-nine per cent of the group will follow your lead and also touch their chin. As humans we are wired to respond to behaviour more than words. *Despite what leaders say, the repeated behaviour of those in senior positions far outweighs the most eloquent rhetoric.*

Mistaken resistance

Resistance arises from anxiety. During change, levels of anxiety and mistrust are high because we have not given sufficient time for people to make their own sense of the context. Passivity and dependence are high because the expectation has been set that leaders have the answers. So we find people are confused and dependent. Both of these states are then easily misunderstood as resistant behaviour – people ask lots of questions, present alternative views or interpretations and disagree with each other. Unfortunately, the typical response to perceived resistance is more 'tell' – explanation and rationale for why something matters and what you need to do. The impact of this misreading is that it creates a hive of activity that adds little value; more time is spent 'managing' resistance. This misunderstanding and misreading of resistance blinds people to the potential of diverse perspectives, at the very time different ideas and perspectives are needed most. Instead of trying to manage people's resistance leaders need to create approaches that make space for people to influence decisions and share different perspectives: in times of change, difference is not only good, it is essential.

The shadow side of telling other people about the sense we have made – what we think is right and what we think they should do – instead of creating a space for them to create their own meaning and decisions on what to do, is:

- anxiety – feeling uncertain and concerned about the future;
- dependence – feeling unable to make decisions and looking to leadership to grant permission for actions;
- mistaken resistance – different interpretations and experiences perceived as the resistance to new ideas and approaches.

Do you recognize these symptoms in your own organization?

How we got here – the rise of the omnipotent leader

Planning and acting as if we can control more than we do is not only tempting, it appears irresistible. Most of us have been taught that if we work hard and focus on what we want to achieve, good outcomes will follow. We are encouraged to focus on what we put 'in'. Traditionally, people recognized as having leadership qualities were identified as those who had the best answers, those who knew what to do (expertise) and could compellingly convince others that they were right (persuasion through reason). Expertise and reason were privileged traits, and the focus was on what an individual could contribute.

Today, in the complex world in which we find ourselves, different traits are demanded. Leaders are under pressure to deliver huge cost savings within a quarter, or come up with new products overnight. Rarely, if ever, will either of these things be achieved through simply telling others what to do. Yet, we find the legacy of our education and expectations pervades. In our executive groups we see leaders struggling with *not* knowing, grappling with stepping back enough to create space for others to contribute. This is not because they don't have the skills to do so. It is based on a fear that it would reflect badly on their leadership capability if they were to do so. It is this perception that keeps us anchored in control mode. It is this legacy of expertise, reason and individual contribution that underpins the tell approach. It makes the tangible first choice because it creates the illusion of being in control. Even when leaders become aware of this legacy and try to shake it off, it is easier said than done.

We should not deny that changing ourselves when others and the system we operate in remain the same is very hard and takes immense courage and focus. We met one leader, Alex, trying to do just this. Alex, a product manager in a faced-paced high street retailer, combined great industry experience with an appetite to challenge himself and change his habits. We worked with him for over 12 months, acting as coach and sounding board as he experimented putting into practice high-quality interaction as the antidote to the tyranny of the tangible.

One Friday at 6.33 am we received an email from Alex asking to reschedule our coaching session. A phone call at 8.30 followed with further detail. An urgent product meeting had been called on Monday and an entire pack of slides had to be digested and a response created for a discussion meeting on the way forward. Back-to-back meetings today already meant weekend working was a given and he just couldn't justify spending an hour with us at this point reflecting on it all. Alex's biggest challenge was how to respond when the system and the expectations of others were contrary to how he was trying to change his behaviour. The content in the form of slides was overwhelming and detracted from real conversation. The focus on preparation and having the answers ready for the meeting made any attempt at facilitating a discussion 'on the way forward' disingenuous at best. Alex took the time to reflect and recognized that the expectations and pressure upon him were luring him back to the tyranny of the tangible. Instead of spending all weekend creating pre-prepared slides based on his own rationale, he gave himself one hour. In that time he called three colleagues, all of whom would be present in the meeting and all of whom had very different perspectives. He asked them one simple question: 'What are the questions we are not asking that we should be?' He used the rest of the time to think of three really great anchor questions that he could keep coming back to in pursuit of a quality dialogue.

> Believing we are right and using reason to prove we are right is the most significant unacknowledged relic of traditional leadership theory.

In summary, let's break down the thinking behind the tell approach to communication. The first assumption is the belief that if you tell people your sense of how things need to be and why, they will see the light. But however brilliantly you articulate your message or however many PowerPoint slides you use, people will rarely if ever see things in the same way. The second assumption is the belief that if only people understood, they would act – anyone who has tried to give up smoking or take up jogging knows only too well this is simply not true. Telling fails because it flies in the face of what it means to be a person – an independent entity with unique experiences and individual interpretations of what is going on, what makes sense and what it is right to do. With help from three philosophers, Epictetus (55–135 AD), David Hume (1711–76) and Jonathan Haidt (b. 1963), we will explore our relationship with communication, control and the creation of meaning.

What philosophy tells us

Epictetus was a Greek stoic philosopher. Born a slave, he became famous for his focus on integrity and self-management. Today, the word stoic is most likely to conjure up images of a rather unemotional, somewhat detached response to the world; in fact this perception has little in common with the roots of the ancient philosophy. At the heart of stoicism is a reminder of how unpredictable the world can be and an encouragement for us to focus on the aspects of life we can control, rather than becoming preoccupied with what we cannot. Stoicism was founded by Zeno of Citium in Cyprus, around 300 BC, and the philosophy later migrated to the home of intellectual and political life in the first century AD – Rome. For Epictetus, stoicism was embedded in the everyday. Philosophy was not a theoretical exercise; it demanded significant practice and serious application. Possibly, it is this that led to such social diversity amongst the ancient stoic philosophers. Hailing from almost every social background imaginable, the three most famous were a Roman Emperor (Marcus Aurelius), a famous playwright and adviser (Seneca) and Epictetus. What unites these three very different people is their shared philosophy of how to live a good life, regardless of the economic or social context they find themselves in.

The stoic philosophy

So, what can we learn from Epictetus and his fellow stoics that might help us with the control orientation implicit in most approaches to communication? Epictetus saw the task of differentiating between what we have control over and what we do not, as one of the most critical in life. This task was deemed so important it even has its own name – the Dichotomy of Control. Epictetus believed that if we are able to focus our attention on what we can control, rather than what we cannot, we ultimately experience less angst, frustration and suffering. The stoics boil down the aspects of life that we can control as beginning and ending with our own thoughts, gestures and responses.

Beyond that, particularly with respect to the thoughts and responses of others, although we may influence, we certainly cannot control or determine them. Epictetus warns us of the perils of behaving as if we can control such things:

> If you regard that... which is not your own as being your own, you'll have cause to lament, you'll have a troubled mind, and you'll find fault with both gods and human beings... (Epictetus, *The Enchiridion* 1).[1]

The warning is clear: the fallacy of control not only leads to inner turmoil, it leads to finding fault with, or blaming others. Ultimately it destroys relationships, the very thing needed for creating meaning and securing long-term commitment to action.

The hardest part of applying the stoic dichotomy of control is recognizing how little really is in our control and choosing to let go of it in how we act: 'To make the best of what is in our power, and take the rest as it occurs.'

As we said earlier, the fallacy of control is so endemic it can be hard to recognize when we are falling into the trap. We have coached numerous leaders who genuinely understand the implications of the tell approach and who are trying hard to change their communication habits but still fall in to prescribing what others should think and feel. Prescription comes in disguise. Just because we are asking questions does not mean we are not telling. We observe it in the form of questions asked in table groups at all staff events – the answers are already known. We see it in transmit-receive communication messages, intended to be one way.

Two questions that can help us spot when we are about to go into tell mode are:

- Do I already know the conclusion I need this conversation to come to?
- Do I become frustrated when people express a different view?

Two reflection questions that can help to avoid the tell trap are:

- What is the source of my fear?
- What can I learn from others that could strengthen our understanding, options and outcomes?

One inspiring CEO we observed talking with his teams recently was modelling what we have come to call 'expert inquirer' mode. At a large all-staff meeting he seated himself among everyone else and simply asked great, open questions. He applied his knowledge and intellect to opening up perspectives and gaining maximum contribution from others. 'Should we be doing more to reduce plastic in our packaging? What do people think?' His role was not to have the answers but to provoke, to get people thinking, to start a conversation where others who were more informed could contribute. Twelve months later the organization was well on its way to launching one of the most innovative 're-use' solutions to reduce packaging waste.

Let's remind ourselves of what we can control and what we cannot. We can control:

- our intentions;
- the process we facilitate (not legislate!);
- our behaviour.

What we cannot control:

- other people's responses to what we say and do;
- the way people experience their context;
- other people's beliefs, emotions and biases;
- other people's actions.

Take a look at the list above. How frequently do your approaches centre on the things we cannot control? What could you do to spend more time:

- reflecting on and sharing your intentions;
- learning about and reflecting on your behaviour;
- facilitating a process that enables others to connect and make their own sense of the context?

Two key lessons from the stoics:

- apply the stoic Dichotomy of Control, and challenge yourself on whether you are focusing on what you can control or things you cannot (and should not);
- focus on facilitating an exceptional process, not controlling a predetermined outcome.

Let's recap. When leaders relay predefined messages, they are working on two assumptions:

1 they can control what people come to understand and believe through reason alone;

2 this understanding of rationale will inspire action.

The first assumption is founded on a fundamental philosophical misconception that meaning can be translated from one person to another through reason. First, with the help of Jonathan Haidt we will come to see that meaning making is an activity that resides in each individual as a person in his or her own right. The second assumption is founded on the philosophical misconception that logic inspires action. With the help of David Hume we will see that ethical action is inspired by passion, developed through a relational process of interaction with others.

Understanding how we come to understand

You have probably been in at least one meeting where consensus and agreement appear to have been reached only for you to later find people huddled around the coffee machine, in the car park, or over dinner, openly sharing their reservations. This process is important, and is our very human way of sense-making – we make sense of information in the context of our understanding of the world. Regardless of how much persuasion, logic and intellect we apply we simply cannot beat the power of our intuition. If something doesn't feel right in our gut we find it difficult, if not impossible to commit to acting on it. The second point to remember is that building our own understanding is a fundamentally social process; we build it in relation with others, particularly those we trust. This is where we will call upon modern moral philosopher Haidt to help us understand the social process of how we make sense.

Understanding as a social process

In the process of developing understanding and deciding how to act we are constantly making decisions.

Haidt presents the idea that when faced with newness the first thing that happens in our minds is a powerful intuitive response. Our intuition fires before we even know it and is likely to be based on links our mind is making between the present and our past. Based on this, we will come to a number of judgements about what it all means. These judgements will include whether this is good or bad, whether we should fear it or embrace it, and how we should act in response. Finally, and only after we have already come to some preliminary conclusions, do we develop a line of reasoning to support our judgements. Haidt seeks to remind us that intuition is the most powerful component in shaping our engagement with new information.

We would add three things to Haidt's thinking. These are the things that the mind will intuitively explore:

1 Emotions – how does this make me feel? We might not know why but we will have a sense of our immediate response.
2 Biases – what am I naturally tuned into at this moment, the opportunities or the threats?
3 Experience – what of a similar nature to this have I seen or experienced before and what was that experience like?

If you pay careful attention to the interactions at the next meeting you find yourself in, you will notice that the majority of the time we appear to be interacting at the level of reasoning. Reason is the international language of business, so it is no surprise that this is the most likely form in which we will share our perspectives. Leaders are less likely to talk openly about their emotions, experiences and biases, and even less so their judgements. And this has a big consequence. If we confront reason with reason, and never explore beneath rationale to the judgements we have made or the emotions, biases and experiences that have led us down that road, we simply hit a brick wall. We will rarely change someone's reasoning on the basis of our own reason alone. We can only do so by starting with an exploration of his or her intuition. If we think about the coffee machine, car park or dinner conversations, what we see is that they are all examples of times when we share and explore our intuition (the emotions, experiences and biases) with people we trust. And this is the key point. We build understanding and will even sometimes change our judgements through sharing our intuition with people whom we trust. When we do this we might see new ways of looking at things. We will not change our judgements through an attack on our reason. We may, in time, concede but this only leads to the façade of agreement accompanied by little follow-through.

So what have we learnt from Haidt?

- We cannot persuade people to change their minds through reason and rationale alone.
- Experiences, emotions and biases are at the heart of how we make sense of anything new.
- Sense-making and creating meaning are iterative processes of relational interaction.

> Real progress requires us to share our fears and instincts openly, not be labelled a resistor for having them.

The road to meaning

Returning to the challenge of enabling individuals to develop their own sense and meaning of the collective challenges in organizations, there are two traps we frequently fall into. The first relates to the time we need to develop meaning – we all have a propensity to dramatically underestimate the journey we have been on. One CEO, frustrated that middle management were not taking the initiative, accepted our challenge that he had almost nine months of time (behind closed doors) to assimilate the context, seek advice and process his thoughts and feelings. However, other people had not and were thus not predisposed to accept his conclusions. He reflected on his journey, recounting the early workshops he had with his consultants that stimulated his thinking, the executive coaching which gave him the space to process it all, and his trusted Chief Strategy Officer with whom he could begin to plan. He acknowledged that it was not just the cognitive but the emotional journey he had been through that mattered most when it came to his ability to act with confidence. His job as CEO was not to have all the answers or to direct and control action through the hierarchy; his job was to create the space for everyone to make their own sense of what collectively needed to happen and find meaning in their contribution to the whole.

When leaders confidently share the why and the what, as they do in our opening Town Hall story, they have more often than not had a significant amount of time to share, iterate and build their responses. They have had time to explore their own intuition and judgements with others whom they trust. This opportunity is rarely available to anyone else. Once the leadership have decided on the way forward it seems unnecessary to repeat the whole sense-making process with others – far better and more effective to save time and simply tell people what they need to do to deliver. Unfortunately this is not the case.

The second trap relates to what happens when action is not forthcoming. Possibly as a consequence of the first trap, energy is refocused on trying to alter the experience of other people – not on understanding *their* experience. This is where 'what's in it for you'-type messaging is most likely to appear. Whilst the intent may be good, to help people see the positives, we only need to reflect on Haidt's thinking to see that reason does not stand a chance against experience. More importantly, this approach diminishes the lived experience of each person as an individual, with their own insights, perspectives and ideas. It stifles contribution.

Commitment to act

Another philosopher who argued that 'sentiment' was more powerful than reason was the Scottish philosopher David Hume (1711–76). Hume was not interested in defining abstract or theoretical tenets that in reality no one lived by; he was fascinated by observing how humans really *are*. In his work *Treatise of Human Nature,* Hume goes against the philosophical grain when he advocates the idea that 'it is not knowing that governs ethical actions but feelings'.[2] This argument is at the core of Sentimentalism or Moral Sense Theory, a philosophical school of thought that argues that the distinction between a moral and an immoral action is discovered through the emotional response to experience, rather than an objective principle or applicable rule.

From observing how people interacted, Hume concluded that *'reason is a slave to the passions'*. By passions, he was talking about what we would identify as our emotions, instincts and desires. By 'slave to' he was referring to the fact that our reason is primarily interested in safeguarding our passions (used as a tool to protect what we care about). If we follow Hume's line of thinking, we begin to see that, far from being the heart of the matter as we might be led to believe through our choices in communication style, reason is post hoc – it is there to justify and keep our passions alive in the face of opposition. By appealing to reason alone we do not inspire action; rather we fail to connect with another's passion and leave them cold to our argument. This is because we neglect to explore the passions of others in the first place. Whereas we might ask what someone thinks, or what their rationale for something is, we are unlikely to have asked about their intentions, wants or feelings. *How people feel and what they want to be known for are drivers of action, not what they are told.*

One of the most famous and shocking reminders of this is the medical statistic that only 10 per cent of patients recovering from a heart bypass operation will make the necessary changes required to their lifestyle to remain healthy. It is unlikely to be a lack of knowledge about the consequences that stops people. It is much more so the fact that significant lifestyle change requires some big changes in identity – who you are and what you are known for. It takes a connection between sentiment and our identity (how we want to be to ourselves and others) to commit to new habits in the form of long-term action:

> Reason alone can never be a motive to any action of the will, and that reason alone can never oppose passion in the direction of the will. Reason *alone* cannot move us to action; the impulse to act itself must come from passion (Hume).

Three lessons from David Hume

- Reason does not drive action – the impulse to act comes from seeking to realize or safeguard our passion.
- Passion emerges from the sharing of experiences and reciprocal encounters with other people.
- Reason can be used as a mask for our passions.

Passions, as Hume referred to them, are not fixed entities; they evolve and change as we go through life and are impacted by our experience of the world. Passion emerges from the sharing of experiences and reciprocal encounters with other people, and we will talk more about this in Chapter 8.

A new way – sense making not sense giving

So far, we have turned to the philosophers to shed some light on the shortcomings of our approaches. Now we will use their wisdom to shape a new path.

Recognizing that we cannot control what people understand, we need to move away from attempting to 'give' sense to others (and alienating them in the process) towards creating opportunities for people to make sense together.

Keith was a client of ours who applied all three of these philosophical lessons to the way he set up a multimillion-pound transformation programme. From the stoics he knew that he could only control the process he facilitated – not the outcome. From Hume he recognized the power of individual passion and from Haidt that intuition comes first and reason last. Keith's job was to dramatically change the working environment for 1,000 employees. It would require a significant cultural shift as offices became open-plan communal areas. Instead of telling people what would happen based on his expertise, experience and very detailed project plan, he recognized the emotional journey he had to take people on, including the levels of fear and anxiety present. Keith understood that he had to connect with people's experience, emotions and biases rather than tell them through reason. One of the most impactful things he did was to give people their own experience of the new – an opportunity to experience positive emotions in the new context. He created a mock-up of the office environment. People could visit, test it out, sit on the new chairs and touch the carpet. It sounds like a small thing but it had a massive impact. Secondly, he didn't use PowerPoint, but let people talk in small groups, inviting their fears and concerns; he wanted not just to hear them so he could create better solutions – he wanted to provide them with the space to process. He was clear on the non-negotiables but asked for help and input on everything else. As a result, people created their own meaning, and fear slowly turned to excitement.

Creating a space where anything is possible

When we asked leaders what they feared if they were to involve their people in defining the future, rather than simply telling them the conclusions they had come to, the overwhelming theme of their answers was a fear that 'anything could happen'. Yet, when we asked the very same leaders what they sought most in their organizations, it was a mix of greater creativity, innovation and agility, things that by their very definition require *anything to be able to happen*. We should be very afraid of anyone who believes and acts as if they are right. To thrive, organizations need, more than ever, a diversity of perspectives, not for everyone to be persuaded of one particular insight, approach or plan. In the next chapter we build on this and explore how our approach to engagement has become confused with our need for people to agree with us – and so demonstrate their commitment.

Summary

For every one of us, the challenge is significant. It requires us to recognize and challenge the rise of the omnipotent leader, responsible for having all the answers and unable to be fully human with the weight of expectation upon them. To recognize and remain aware of what we cannot control and let go of it. To focus our energies on facilitating a great process – embracing emergence as something that really does mean that anything can happen. When people have the space to make their own meaning they also define the path that leads to collective action.

Rather than constantly telling others what we think, we would create more human workplaces where people, ideas and performance flourish if we could embrace the virtue that we see things differently.

Questions

1 To what extent are your energies and activities focused on the things you can control (your intentions, behaviour and the processes you can facilitate)?

2 How often do you take the time to dig deeper and understand other people's intuitions (their emotions and experiences)?

3 How can you show up as a vulnerable, fallible leader who doesn't have all the answers and through doing so, permit others to do the same?

Notes

1 Epictetus (c. AD 125) *The Enchiridion*, various editions
2 Hume, D (1738) *A Treatise of Human Nature*

08

From engagement to encounter

In the previous chapter we saw the need to challenge the conventional approach to communication and create the space for people to make their own meaning in support of their objectives. In this chapter we will turn to the related topic of engagement and see once again that we are looking in the wrong place for the answer. For a workplace to feel human we need to have genuine connection with others.

With the help of the philosopher Martin Buber we will explore how we need to shift from measuring engagement and treating people as a means to an end, to making space in our minds and diaries for encounter. We will see the damage that is done when we treat people as a means to an end and seek only to 'engage' them in our agenda. We will unravel the issues and challenges to see that the job of leadership is not to engage people or measure their commitment, but to create a space for engaged people to encounter others in a way that is truly transformational to both the individual and the organization.

The annual engagement survey

Let us start by visiting an organization we worked with on this challenge.

The annual engagement report finally landed in the inbox of the top team. The CEO was relieved to finally have the data. It had been a turbulent year of change and plummeting morale. Sixteen weeks had passed since the majority of the company had submitted their answers to 50-plus questions, persuaded to do so only by desperate pleas from HR to complete the survey – 'Your views are really important to us!'

Amongst the plethora of bar charts and indistinguishable data collations from various departments, one overwhelming statistic stood out. Confidence in the top team was 32 per cent. What! Only 32 per cent of people consider us, the leadership team, capable of providing the direction required. The rest of the report became a blur. The CEO called an urgent, confidential meeting with the head of HR and his team. An action plan was required. What could be done? Advice was sought. Consultants were consulted. Time went by. Meanwhile the rest of the organization forgot about it. Until, several months later, a sanitized version of the report was published along with the announcement that the leadership team were committed to achieving upper-quartile engagement scores within two years. A range of new KPIs would be established to ensure improvement.

For most organizations, conducting an annual engagement survey is as commonplace as having the values emblazoned on the walls. The act of conducting such surveys is seen as a measure of the seriousness with which the engagement issue is being treated by senior management. And the industry is booming, with more players joining the market each year. In 2018, LinkedIn announced their investment of US $400 million to acquire Glint, a leader in employee engagement. The question is, what impact is all this actually having on levels of engagement?

In this chapter, with the help of Martin Buber, we will look at the challenge of engagement through a philosophical lens. We will explore the intentions that underpin the way engagement is thought about and integrated into leadership practice. We will encourage you to reflect on how this topic shows up in your life and work. Having explored the philosophical perspective, we will apply our learning to some of the classic approaches to engagement and see how, unfortunately, they only act to undermine engagement. Here, we offer an alternative view. Instead of focusing on how engaged others are in our agenda, we will see that we would do better, for the flourishing of people, ideas and performance, to develop our ability to fully encounter one another. We will see that encounter is an altogether different quality of connection. Encounter goes to the core of who we are; it is deeply relational – it is the definition of engagement.

To begin, let us return to our opening story and step into the shoes of those involved. The leadership team are no doubt feeling the pressure, acutely responsible but uncertain about what steps to take. What can they do? What should they do? They need to be seen to be acting but where to start? They eventually (inadvertently) employ the same mechanisms that got them the result that they are trying to change. They try to manage their way to better engagement scores on the basis that you get what you measure. They set up engagement KPIs to contain the anxiety without realizing that the KPIs create anxiety, undermine engagement and slow or block progress on the causes we share.

Let's think about the HR team. First, they had to convince the organization to complete the survey – not an easy job given the cynicism that the last survey left. Next, they became the bearers of bad news to the leadership team, working day and night making the report as palatable as possible. The delay in sharing this year's results is certainly doing nothing for their reputation. Exhausted and at the frontline of it all, they feel berated and unsupported. And the rest of the organization? At best, people experience the survey process as a distraction; at worst it is deeply undermining of what it means to contribute to something you care about.

So why this approach?

The most-cited rationale for the purpose of engagement surveys is to determine 'the level of an employee's psychological investment in the organization'. But from Aristotle to Kant, philosophers would argue that engagement simply *is* the human condition. Anthropologist and author Joseph Henrich would say it is exactly this ability for our minds to socially interconnect with one another that is the secret of our success as a species. Our minds need to be engaged with other minds.

As people, we are hard-wired to make a meaningful contribution; we want to feel part of something bigger than ourselves. We are at our most human when we are working to achieve something together.

The focus on engagement

Engagement, particularly stakeholder engagement, is a core component of the traditional business school curriculum. We are told it is the key to translating a great global strategy into tangible local action. It is the foundation for achieving cultural change and creating agile, innovative organizations. We, the authors, spend a lot of our time coaching and advising teams and leaders on these challenges. We find engagement is at the top of the CEO agenda, whether it be how to create connections between colleagues across the organization, or, like the CEO in our introduction to this chapter, how to convince 68 per cent of the organization to have confidence in the leadership team. The focus on engagement makes sense – we recognize we simply cannot get things done alone.

Is your agenda worthy?

Recently, in a workshop, we ran an exercise where participants were invited to use physicality to represent their relationship with a concept or person. We asked the participants to reflect on and represent their relationship with the newly proposed organizational strategy. The strategy was represented by a chair placed in the centre of the room, and we asked participants to take a position relative to the chair to express their feelings towards the strategy. One participant stood as far away as physically possible from the chair, earnestly looking out of the window with her back to it (and everyone else).

What followed in the discussion provided a particularly interesting insight into how engagement is processed. Immediately, she was barraged with questions. Why did she feel like this? Was she aware of others who felt like this? Was she planning a coup? Exploring the group's reaction revealed two things. First, there was a marked reluctance to accept and learn from what had just been very vividly revealed – in this case the sense of separateness, represented by position, being expressed by their colleague. Second, the desire amongst the rest of the group to quickly fix, mitigate and manage what they saw as total 'disengagement' – which of course is only one interpretation. The alternative, opening it up and engaging in the opportunity, to explore everyone's interpretation, including the person of attention's, to learn something that might enhance the strategy itself, was passed by. As we explored in Chapter 7, we often resort to habits that undermine learning when we are under pressure to deliver. We relate to emotion as an unruly force to be put aside so we can focus on content, or 'facts', to prevent our plans being derailed.

During the workshop break, the head of business development and the head of HR began appealing to us, the facilitators. How can we 'engage' our colleague in the new future? As a member of the leadership team she (the participant 'distancing' herself from the strategy) *should* be engaged and committed to this, said one in despair. Our response was instinctive. Why? Why should she? What followed was silence. Neither the head of business development nor the head of HR could answer why. The dilemma that they were contemplating was, should we be trying to convince, or should we be trying to learn?

Do we confront this dilemma enough? Are we aware of the moments when we demand someone's engagement in our agenda as if we have the right to? Demanding and learning are very different ways of relating. The first, to demand or to convince, is grounded in the idea that we are right, which, as explored in Chapter 4, is rare and at best momentary. The second, to learn, is grounded in the idea of experimentation, to consciously and persistently test our truth hypothesis through encounter and feedback. In Chapter 4 we propose that strategy is a series of experiments in which we learn and adjust our beliefs. In other words, we continuously embark on a journey of learning – of seeking the truth. If you ran a similar exercise, using physicality and metaphor to reveal feelings and differences in your own context, what might you learn about how others experience things and how could you behave to maximize your learning and the learning of others?

One of the exercises we regularly use is to confront teams with a challenge that at first seems to have an obvious answer which subsequently turns out to be wrong. One participant, a finance director, was convinced until the end that his answer was right. It turned out he was wrong. Ever since, he has been retelling the story to colleagues: 'I have learned that even when I am convinced I am right, I need to remember that I could be wrong and I need to listen to and explore all interpretations and points of view'.

The trouble with 'buy-in'

The term 'engagement' is often used synonymously with the phrase 'buy-in', the process of getting people to support and commit to an initiative being driven, usually at pace, from the top, with clear milestones and business benefits. The common question is how to attain 'buy-in' from other stakeholders, particularly those who will have an effect on the overall outcome, and how to engage the wider organization in the leadership team's vision.

A few years ago, one of us worked closely as an adviser to the head of transformation at a global retailer. She was passionate and committed to her job and she ran a large team of equally enthusiastic, intelligent, high-potential people. Early on it became apparent that she kept a mega spreadsheet which seemed to drive her 'engagement' activities across the business. When we inquired about its purpose we discovered that it listed every senior manager across the organization and gave them an associated RAG status. For those not familiar with such project management jargon, RAG stands for RED-AMBER-GREEN and is used to denote the status in relation to progress of an objective. In this case the objective was 'buy-in'. Think for a moment of a project going on in your organization. Can you imagine being 'RAG-ed' today? How would you fare? Suppose you are considered RED based on the challenges you posed in a recent meeting. Does this give any insight at all into what you are offering in terms of your energy, curiosity and contribution? How would it feel if this spreadsheet were to be found and people, their passion and their commitment reduced to a RAG status? The spreadsheet was of course founded on the idea of engagement as a binary process of convincing others to agree; identifying those who were problematic and building confidence on the basis of those who seemed supportive. This is not a foundation for transformation and learning. This is a risk management approach.

Engagement is not the problem

And so we arrive at our provocation to learn – engagement is not the problem. To be engaged is to be human. Apart from when we are mentally stretched beyond our limits, we humans are always engaged. Engaged in others, our family, our friends, our neighbours, our community and our causes. The challenge we face in our organizations is not that people are not engaged. In a study we conducted in over 100 organizations, the most frequently selected words to describe how people felt, from a list of over 30, were engaged, committed and proud. In the same study, people were asked to select the five dominant behaviours in their organization, again from a list of over 30. In over 80 per cent of cases the dominant behaviours were hierarchical, controlling and conforming. Engagement surveys reinforce the idea that there is a problem and that there is a management solution. The problem is not a need for more management control, it is an absence of leadership. The hierarchical, controlling approach is getting in the way of engaged people contributing.

A quick recap:

- We treat engagement as a state to be managed rather than understanding it as the human condition – a need to feel connected to others and to our causes.
- We mistake anything other than complete agreement as 'disengagement'.
- We have created an engagement industry that acts as a disservice to our desire to connect people and causes to make great stuff happen.
- We focus too much on trying to convince others rather than learning from them.

What does philosophy tell us?

To help us apply a philosophical lens to the challenge of engagement, we are going to explore the ideas of Martin Buber (1878–1965), an Austrian-born, Israeli-Jewish philosopher best known for his writings on the topic of dialogue. Buber was inspired by Nietzsche and Kant to study philosophy but rejected the title of philosopher, proclaiming he was not interested in ideas but personal experience. Human existence, particularly interactions, feature in Buber's book *I and Thou*.[1] In this text published in 1923, Buber sets out his idea that there are two fundamentally different ways to relate to and interact with the world. The first mode of interaction Buber calls 'I-It'. In the 'I-It' mode we relate to the world and other people as an objective observer. We are consciously or subconsciously focused on assimilating knowledge that can be used for our own ends, always in relation to our own context or objectives. We experience others as a means to our ends. In this I-It mode, we are gathering data through the senses and organizing it so it can be utilized by reason. Of course, this way of being is demanded of us a lot of the time. I-It is absolutely necessary for survival. A lot of the time we simply need to get things done, fix things, be able to anticipate and avoid disaster. When we ask what type of tyre we should buy for our bike or whether someone can fix our computer we are in the realm of I-It. What does all this mean for me?

The second mode of interacting with the world, Buber terms I-Thou; this is the realm of relation. Here we are active participants, always in relationship with the other, not separated from them. We encounter the other in their entirety and not simply as a subset of individual qualities. Most importantly, both parties are altered by the encounter; there is reciprocity, mutual learning, transformation. It is in I-Thou, through relation, that we develop our character and work out who and how we want to be in the world.

What would Buber have to say about the dominant organizational approach to engagement? For sure, he would see it as 'I-It' interaction. The use of engagement surveys and the preoccupation with 'buy-in' are built on a core of defining and assimilating the individual into a series of component parts. Some of the questions are aimed at synthesizing how committed a person is to our organization's direction. How much are they putting in? Will they stay? Do the leadership team have their support and loyalty? How much energy do they have? And in the case of 'buy-in', what does an individual think and feel about our plans? How critical is their view to making our agenda possible? What skills, qualities and capabilities do they bring? What do the answers to these questions mean for me, for the strategy, for the team? This dissemination would worry Buber greatly. In his writing he warned that we are increasingly living in an 'it' world, and whilst recognizing that I-It is an imperative to functioning, when it becomes the dominant mode of interaction we risk alienation.

We can identify a similar theme in the 'telling' approach to communication that we reflected on in Chapter 7. 'Telling' others what they need to understand and how they need to act is an I-it form of interaction that acts only to separate, alienate and inhibit action.

An alternative – encounter

So what can you do? We need to switch our focus from the pursuit of engagement. In this section we take a look at the process of encounter and how it differs from engagement. When we encounter each other we learn from each other, we share an experience, we are changed through our interaction. When we engage with someone the focus is on purpose, on an outcome, on the reason for our engagement, on convincing. Typically, when we talk about the need for more engagement in our organizations, we mean we want people to be more committed to, supportive of and active in pursuing *our* agenda. An encounter is an unplanned, often unexpected experience through which we are changed. If what we seek is transformation and co-creation, to mutually benefit from our innate desire to be engaged with others and our causes, we need to understand how to be open to and create space to encounter each other. Instead of focusing on how engaged we, or others, are, we would do better to reflect on and work on moments of encounter. How we encounter others and how they encounter us – moment to moment, every single day.

Buber argues that encounter, being in I-Thou relation, is the primary state for humans and the answer to our feeling of alienation. We can think of encounter as moments of reciprocity, of being seen and being heard – moments that Buber speaks of in which all parties have the capacity to be transformed. In our organizational context, it means a shift from thinking about what information I can garner and how I might use it, to meeting someone as an entity, an encounter in which the unexpected and new may take hold. In encounter, we co-create. We transform ourselves and our ideas.

A colleague of ours, Professor Megan Reitz, talks about the difference between 'being and seeming' with respect to relational leadership.[2] The realm of encounter requires us to be, rather than seem to be. Being requires us to be in relation. To be in the moment. Accessing the richness of our thinking and feeling and giving the same access to others. It is not static, attained by refining particular traits. It is a constant process of momentary relational interaction. Seeming is the selective projection of an image. It gives little access to the source of learning and transformation. Rather, it narrows the field of interaction and disconnects us from our experience. This is the thing we observe leaders struggling with most; how to let go of the projection of how they should be, to let go of the need to convince, and to embrace the transformation power of encounter. In a world dictated by to-do lists and overflowing inboxes there is an understandable urge for things to be completed, ticked off, 'done'.

During a workshop we ran for a group of leaders in a large UK organization we had been asked to focus on helping them hone their skills with respect to building relationships. We created a number of scenarios where participants would meet an actor as a stakeholder relevant to the task they needed to pursue. Two things struck us: first, how the majority of people approached the meeting as a transaction. They didn't seek to understand the person, they sought to identify and secure commitment in terms of how the person could help them. The second thing we observed was how many people felt they had 'messed up' their interaction with the actor and then experienced a desire to avoid the person thereafter. When we explored it, the participants held a view that the meeting was done, there was no going back, it was a one-off event that had not gone so well but nonetheless was over. It had been ticked off, much like a task on a to-do list. But being in relation is not a series of events, it is a perpetual dynamic state. We explored with the group what it would be like to layer on a new interaction, share the emotional challenge of what was going on for them with the other person and explore different ways of relating. A relationship can be constantly developed, nuanced and enhanced if we focus on being rather than seeming.

To recap again:

- Engagement, commitment and pride are not the problem, they are integral to the human condition and are always present in functional human beings.
- We need to shift our focus from engagement to encounter; to create space in our minds and our diary to embrace the unexpected that stems from an open, genuine and full-hearted expression of who we are and acceptance of who others are.
- We need to remind ourselves of what the Dalai Lama said: 'We are not human doings, we are human beings'. We need to be present in the moment, to let others see and experience who we are and seek to know and experience others as they are.

How can we embrace encounter?

Changing our mindset from engagement to encounter is challenging in today's organizations with the pressure on targets and individual achievement. But it is possible. One of us authors has been coaching Mark, a senior leader in a global bank. Mark's team had scored poorly in the annual engagement survey. In particular, they didn't score well in creating a link between the organizational strategy and their objectives. This was causing Mark a great deal of stress as numbers for the quarter were also down. As his bosses began asking for progress updates he spent more and more time in meetings with his team. With more Skype 121s and a weekly face-to-face team meeting, his diary became jammed with back-to-back meetings.

When we began our coaching sessions, Mark talked earnestly about how he had increased face-to-face time with the team in a bid to improve the situation. We asked how he was finding it. He expressed his frustration at constantly having to run to catch up, constantly being in meetings. No time to think. We talked about what engagement meant to him. We asked him about times when he had felt connected and engaged with others. It was hard for him to find an experience of this at work. As a consequence of this discussion, Mark decided to experiment. He reduced the number of meetings he was in by one third. He created more time to think. He scrapped the 121s and found ways to connect with individuals informally and proactively. He asked one to join him for a working session on a new project. He went for a walk around St James's Park with another. He learnt a lot about his team. People loved their work and they were committed to the organization. They worked far longer hours than he knew, mitigating issues that never reached him. They were engaged! During this time, he created space for encounter. Not just space in his diary but space in his mind – time to be, as opposed to not enough time to do. In the working sessions he found himself listening more, speaking less. He found himself thinking what would Kris or Sam say? Can we get their voice in the room? Mark stopped trying to engage with people or trying to force them to engage with him. He focused instead on encounter, on being with others and allowing others to be with him. The impact was considerable. In the last session of his coaching Mark shared how reframing engagement not as a condition to be achieved but as simply being able to relate in the moment had changed both his numbers and how he felt about his team. Why? Because he and his team had started learning and creating together.

Through the executive programmes we run, we have so many examples, like Mark, of the power of encounter to accelerate learning and bring about transformation. Whether working with people from across one organization, or on open programmes with 50 people from across the world, from different cultures, with different roles, from different sectors and organizations, we see transformation through encounter. We see people beginning as strangers and leaving as friends. We witness spontaneous, meaningful conversation. What starts as a collection of separate individuals within days becomes a connected community of learners. In the groups that come from the same organization we hear wonderful stories. People who have known *of* each other for years will reveal to the group (often over a dinner) their trepidation on day one about being in a group with the head honcho and then their elation that she is, in fact, a person just like them. Leaders in strategy admit that they got 'people in IT wrong'. They are not blockers, they are 'trying to make this happen too'. There are many more stories like these. When people are able to 'be' and not 'seem', human connection and engagement is abundant; in the right conditions it naturally flourishes.

The ingredients that lead to such encounters and need to be actively facilitated by leadership have become clear to us over the many programmes, clients and communities we have worked with. We have summarized them here.

- **Being present**. The time people spend together is intense and focused on each other. They are not distracted or interrupted by other demands. Meetings and emails take a back seat. They have time to listen, so they can be and not only do.

- **Person, not role**. Participants show up as themselves, not as their role. Hopes, fears, strengths, vulnerabilities are all to be shared, related to and supported. They are being, not seeming.

- **Incomplete**. No one is the finished article. Leaders come prepared to let their guard down, to be curious about their shortcomings and their impact on others. In so doing they unlearn bad habits and learn new ways of being that serve them better.

- **Relation, not agreement.** Learning is more important than agreement. People contribute with conviction but in the full knowledge they could be wrong, that others could be right and we could all be wrong. We are fallible.

Implications for leadership

Buber argues that encounter is the answer to our alienation, the antidote to our reliance on I-It interaction. Encounter is also the way in which we as individuals transform – through relation with others who have seen and heard us and who we have seen and heard. So how can we apply some of this thinking to our context of leadership?

First we need to recognize that encounter cannot be premeditated. Encounter is about the unexpected. If we want to benefit from the learning that stems from the unexpected we need to create the conditions where we are open and have the space in our lives to be part of it. This requires being fully present, connecting with the words and emotions of others and of ourselves as they are expressed, amended and re-expressed, not filtered and reshaped by what we want to or are prepared to hear. It means sharing what is going on for us – emotions, thoughts, worries, dreams.... It means discarding stereotypes, giving up predicting how others will respond, what they think, or what they can offer us. In highly organized transactional silo-based organizations, we very quickly develop narratives about others. We categorize them and soon create a single narrative that applies to anyone and everyone in each category. The trouble with IT people is... well, he would say that, he's in marketing.... Encounter happens through dialogue, between people not categories; it needs space and openness.

John is CEO of a social enterprise focused on helping people with learning disabilities find meaningful, productive work. Earlier in his career, John was the organization's IT manager, with no aspiration to be CEO. The organization at that time had 500 computers across 90 buildings and an estimated 700 computer users. The IT department had three staff, including John. It was a very busy department and the majority of the computer users in the organization were not proficient in IT.

For several years John had been asked by colleagues to consider supporting a person with a learning disability in the IT department. He persistently declined, thinking, in his words:

- it is not the role of the IT department to provide direct support ('we support others to support others');
- I have no direct experience in supporting someone with a learning disability ('I don't know what this looks like');
- we are too busy to take someone into the department and train them ('this is adding to the workload');
- what skills does he bring to this busy department? ('He has a learning disability, how can he add value?)

His colleagues did not give up, and one day they presented John with a very specific request. Again in John's words:

> I was told that there was a person, Robert, with a learning disability, who was a camera enthusiast, a gadget lover, and a gamer. Robert was 21 and he wanted to work in IT. He was acutely shy and withdrawn. He had other additional but minor co-existing health difficulties.

After several meetings with Robert's support team, John was finally persuaded: 'At that time, I had to complete a manual audit of all computer equipment, including gadgets such as phones and cameras.' John takes up the story of what happened:

> I met Robert on his arrival on his first day, and we went and had a cup of tea. We chatted about interests, hobbies and other topics to understand Robert's skill base in IT. I spent the full week building a relationship with Robert, developing an audit tool with him that he could use, setting out a project schedule with him in daily detail, and introducing him to the staff he would be meeting in the first few weeks of his audit work. I discovered his wicked sense of humour and intolerance of staff who were not proficient in IT. We were going to get on great!
>
> Over the following weeks, Robert began to fix small computer problems for staff as he was auditing. I had set up a few of these types of interactions over the first week of auditing to build his confidence in speaking with staff, but then it happened organically and by happenstance – a problem in printing a document as Robert was

recording serial numbers, etc. During this time, I treated Robert as a member of staff in the team. The only additional support I provided was a meeting with him every morning to confirm his work for the day and a meeting with him in the afternoon to check his progress. I made sure he knew who to lunch with each day (pre-arranged based on location) and told him where I would be in case of emergency.

After five months the audit was complete. Robert had grown in confidence and enjoyed interacting with staff. I set out a new project upgrading versions of Microsoft Windows on computers, again necessary and relevant, but more challenging. We spent a week developing a large checklist with supporting instruction sheets to work through a complete upgrade for a computer. Robert refined his document by trial and error, practising with spare computers in the department for the next two weeks, and then he worked out on the live computing environment. Over time he became ever more skilled, started answering the phone, supported staff in all manner of topics, joked with staff, laughed at some who should not be allowed near a computer, and functioned like a regular member of the IT department. His health problems escalated from time to time but were manageable with some rest. I treated him as a fellow staff member. In the language of social role valorization, he was now an IT engineer.

The encounter changed both John and Robert. John experienced someone he had previously categorized as having a learning disability, as a capable person. A person who touched him, who challenged him, who surprised him. This experience was the beginning of John seeing himself as not just an IT person but as someone with a passion about the service the organization provided and with the ambition, one day, to play a much more pivotal role. He is now CEO. Robert saw himself not just as a gamer but as an IT engineer.

The real work

The authors were called by the vice president of a global retailer. He needed help. His team were not aligned on how to lead the business towards the future vision. How could he get them engaged and instigating action – fast? With some reluctance that it wasn't tangible enough, our proposal – six months of team coaching with the group of eight – began. We were solely focused on their interactions with each other, as we knew these would be reflected and amplified throughout the organization. During the first session, the group found it virtually impossible to reflect on or notice their interactions; they were so focused on delivering their KPIs and what they needed from each other. Each member of the team was exceptionally talented in their field, be it quality, supply chain or sourcing, but they were not a team. They were in hunker down mode. During the third session, we began to see some people emerging from behind their roles. The conversation gradually shifted from targets and delivery to fears and vulnerabilities. Gender, status and privilege begun to come up. As facilitators we were slowly creating the conditions for encounter. For people to 'be' themselves and to explore what was happening between them, moment to moment. It took another few sessions and lots of work in between before we reached a tipping point epitomized by a particularly poignant contribution from Sergio, the head of supply chain:

> I've been pretty outspoken about this before; as you know, I didn't get why we were doing this at the beginning. I was frustrated about how we were not doing *anything*, not even looking at the numbers. I thought these sessions were navel gazing and I wanted to get on with the real work. *Now I get it, this **is** the real work. How we connect* is *the job of leadership, and the quality of our interaction is the work we should be focusing on.*

Changing our practices

Much of what we have talked about in our earlier chapters gets in the way of encounter. Our approach to communication, our approach to strategy, our approach to empowerment. If we challenge our thinking and change the questions we ask and our practices and habits in each of these areas of organizational life, we will go a long way to creating an environment in which encounter will flourish. But we can go further. Here are some ideas on how to open up our minds and create space for encounter, to relate to others and create a common cause to make great things happen.

- **Reframe meetings:**
  - Halve the number of regular meetings in your diary. Or consider eliminating all of them.
  - Get rid of agendas for any meeting that you hold. Start each meeting with the question, 'What's going on for you?' Do not seek agreement, seek to understand others' perspectives and go from there.
  - Trust that each person will use learning to strengthen their contribution and in so doing improve collective performance.
  - Consider that if you cannot trust people, they're not the right people, rather than you not having the right agenda.
- **Be:**
  - stop and talk to the people you bump into;
  - set about bumping into people;
  - learn about the person, not just their role;
  - turn off your phone, switch off your email.
- **Share:**
  - what you observe, how you are feeling, what you are thinking;
  - what you're doing;
  - what excites you and what frightens you;
  - what you would like to happen;
  - ask others to share the same.

Sakis Kotsantonis, the CEO and founding partner of strategy consultancy firm KKS, spoke with us about the endemic meeting culture we are up against and how he is determined to do things differently within his own firm: 'The quickest endorphin hit is a calendar invite and an empty slot – it *feels* productive!'

But in KKS it is different. When you walk in, you feel the energy bouncing off the walls. There are no glass meeting rooms but people are constantly interacting, sat together in small groups working on a project or in pairs planning a proposal. Regular 121s are banned, spontaneous ones the norm. Everyone considers time their most precious asset. As CEO, Sakis recognizes that regular ritualistic meetings more often than not add no personal or business value and act only to take people away from their shared purpose, what they are co-creating with colleagues or clients. People become frustrated. They switch off. Sakis is clear about how he is trying to create a different kind of encounter: 'When meetings happen, the question is always how will this conversation help us? What can we learn?' In this organization it is not being invited to 'that meeting' that matters, it's the quality of the contribution you make within it that counts.

Being present – a necessity for encounter

Research highlights that being centred can help us to become more mindful and better able to respond rather than react. It is also critical in helping us be more present, more able to **be** in the current moment. This includes not just being present with others but also being more present to ourselves. One of the challenges we have with being present to ourselves stems back to 1641 and the French philosopher René Descartes. In *Meditations on First Philosophy*, Descartes outlined his concept of dualism, the separation of the mind and body. His thesis concludes that the body cannot think; he later epitomized this with the now-famous 'Cogito ergo sum' – 'I think, therefore I am'.[3] This mind-body or head-heart separation has provided a foundation stone for much of how we are taught to think about ourselves and the world. Particularly in the west, we are encouraged to pay more attention to the rational and cognitive. The commonplace phrase, 'mind over matter', even implies we can use this separation to overcome our emotions. But we are not just our minds; the body can 'know' in a just as powerful, albeit different way. We only have to think of falling in love or meeting a future friend to recognize that our body (somatic senses) has the capacity to know in a *more than* rational way. Privileging the cognitive to such an extent makes being *fully* aware of how we are – the somatic states that accompany our emotions – difficult. Somatic knowing is not something that words can necessarily do justice to, but if we think of times we have felt fearful or anxious we can see that we only come to cognitively know this through 'data' from our body – the butterflies or the tightening of our chest. It is only then that we can notice and inquire into what this may 'be about'.

In most of the organizations we work with, people are 10 times more likely to share their thoughts than their feelings. 'I think therefore I am' has created an unhelpful separation of the body and the mind. We consistently observe leaders being more at ease in the cognitive realm – talking about what they know rationally (amassed through considerable expertise) to the detriment of noticing and sharing how they feel. Developing the ability to be centred can support becoming more aware of our whole selves, and can help rebalance the attention we give to the cognitive and rational.

Bain & Company's research on centeredness is a good resource for those wishing to develop the practice.[4] There are three things to pay attention to:

1 settling: bringing total awareness to ourselves – our breathing, sensations, feelings, impulses;

2 sensing: naming possible emotions related to physical sensations as they appear;

3 shifting: being a neutral observer in relation to this awareness.

As with everything, practice is the key but even experimenting with the three steps before a big meeting or at the beginning of the day can have a significant impact on our ability to be fully present with ourselves – the precursor to engagement.

Summary

When it comes to engagement, you don't get what you measure, you reap what you sow. People engage with people and causes – not targets. By focusing on targets, we disengage people. Leadership is not directing people to certain outcomes, controlling how they do things, or persuading them to conform with new ways of doing things. Leadership is about connecting people through their common causes to work together and learn from each other. The preoccupation with engagement in organizations is misguided; engagement is not the problem. People are naturally, instinctively predisposed to be engaged, committed and proud. We engage with others and with our causes all the time – it is the human condition. Instead of trying to engage others, the role of leadership is to facilitate encounter. To encounter someone is to meet them as they are.

Questions

1 Do you know the story of the people you work with, where they have come from, their drama and their deliberations? If not, start asking. To know someone's story is to know them as a person.

2 How could you structure your meetings to allow people to become fully present and fully able to express their feelings as much as their ideas?

3 How can you ensure you always come away from a conversation knowing more about yourself, about the other person and about the world?

In the next chapter, we explore the moral dilemmas that we face when we wean ourselves off the platitudes of corporate values statements and confront the tensions between our real values: the values embedded through our different stories.

Notes

1 Buber, M (1923) *I and Thou* (translated in 1958 by Ronald Gregor Smith), various editions

2 Reitz, M (2015) *Dialogue in Organizations: Developing relational leadership*, Palgrave Macmillan

3 Descartes, R (1685) *Principals of Philosophy*, various editions

4 Horwitch, M and Whipple Callahan, M (2016) The science of centredness, Bain & Co [online] https://www.bain.com/insights/the-science-of-centeredness/ (archived at https://perma.cc/95AK-RC53)

09

Values and ethical pluralism

In this chapter we will explore with the help of two philosophers how the focus on defining corporate values is both harmful to the individual and risky to the organization. We will see how values have taken on a life more as behavioural rules to be regulated than as virtues to guide morality. Throughout this chapter we will unravel the issues and challenges to see that behaving morally is much more than compliance. We will uncover the enormous ethical risk we run when we outsource our moral conscience, in the form of values, to the corporation, instead of owning our responsibility for acting as moral citizens. We will conclude that to overcome the learned moral helplessness that results from the focus on organizational values, the job of leadership is not to spend time defining and sharing what values people should hold, but to recognize the dilemmas inherent in doing the right thing and hold a space in which they can be explored.

In business we rarely confront choices that can be framed as good versus evil. Most choices – and what makes them difficult and stressful – are situations where we feel forced to choose between competing versions of what is right and good. We might hold care and honesty as sacred values, but can we always be both caring and honest at the same time? In other words, values and morality are by their nature in tension.

How can these moral dilemmas be reconciled? This is the real 'values problem' in business. They cannot be resolved by simply abiding by rules to 'care' or 'be honest' but by finding genuinely original ways of combining seemingly conflicting values to form actions in new and unique situations. Ethical conduct is discovered as we live; it cannot be entirely predefined.

This book is about humanizing how we work. If there is no moral freedom in our organization then it cannot be a human workplace. Our notion of what is right and wrong is a fundamental part of what makes us human and individual. People have values, organizations cannot.

> Corporate value statements encourage managers to outsource their conscience to the moral custodians of the enterprise, rather than take personal responsibility for acting as moral citizens. Learned moral helplessness is the result.

A plethora of values

Walking into the glamorous foyer of one of the leading investment banks in Canary Wharf, the visitor is greeted by an elegant signboard above the reception desk proclaiming the bank's values:

- Putting clients first.
- Doing the right thing.
- Leading with exceptional ideas.
- Giving back.

They seem to be saying this with no hint of irony or self-parody. At first glance, it comes across as a sincere statement of moral intent.

On reflection, however, there is something banal and naïve about this expression of the bank's true beliefs, however well intentioned and authentically expressed. Imagine the opposite values being proposed:

- Putting clients last.
- Doing the wrong thing.
- Following with mediocre ideas.
- Taking back.

This would be nonsensical, of course. But if so, then stating the 'sensible' values is simply to state moral truisms. The bank's much-vaunted 'values statement' turns out to be vacuous.

Would it be an exaggeration to say that most corporate value statements are similarly empty of content? Take the following examples:

- The best people (Accenture).
- Genuine (Adobe).
- Integrity (American Express).
- Outperform (The Honest Company).
- Accept and delegate responsibility (Ikea).
- Do the right thing (Nike).

No company would choose to employ the worst people, or set out to underperform against its competitors, or focus on failure, so why go to such lengths to state the opposite? Why make such a fuss proclaiming what everyone in a company knows full well to be part and parcel of doing a good job? It is intrinsic to business that excellence is preferable to mediocrity, that every job entails responsibility, that success demands a degree of innovation, that collaborative skills are valuable, and that trust, integrity and honesty are core values in any collective pursuit.

The problem here is that these grand notions are so ill defined and so open to interpretation that employees may feel none the wiser – or no more confident or careful – for knowing that these are the ideals against which their deeds are to be assessed.

What is more, many values that have always been important to human beings are almost entirely absent in values statements – values that are highly relevant to creating a humanized workplace:

- Of the four so-called cardinal values – prudence, courage, temperance and justice – only courage makes a regular appearance.
- Values such as honour, kindness, mercy, patience, humility and generosity get remarkably few mentions.
- 'Fun' is sometimes included – but always at the end, and invariably with an exclamation mark, as though it were a slightly naughty afterthought.

- The irony that normally accompanies expressions of human vanity is almost entirely absent.

At the other end of the spectrum, there are some highly eccentric and witty statements of intent:

- You can be serious without a suit (Google).
- Create fun and a little weirdness (Zappos).
- Di-bear-sity, Colla-bear-ate, Cele-bear-ate (Build-a-Bear).
- Don't be evil (Google).

These bring a smile to the face and lighten what can sometimes come across as high-minded tosh. Then there are some genuinely distinctive and noble aspirations:

- Building communities (Four Seasons Hotels and Resorts).
- Reaching every person on the planet (Twitter).
- Striving to create economic opportunities for those who have been denied them and to advance new models of economic justice that are sustainable and replicable (Ben and Jerry's Ice Cream).

The issue here, perhaps, is how seriously are these causes being taken? How great is the gap between rhetoric and reality, and how realistic are the chances of achievement?

What is the problem to which a value statement is the solution?

The issue, as philosophers would see it, is that value statements, for all their piety, do not address what is morally problematic in the day-to-day life of an executive. Most moral problems in business present themselves as **dilemmas,** that is, as issues where values are in conflict.

Choices in business are occasionally choices between good and bad, in which case the standard values statement, particularly if accompanied by sanctions for non-adherence, may well serve a useful purpose. More often, however, the moral choices that are routine in business, that are most problematic, and that call for the greatest clarity in their handling, are choices between different versions of what counts as 'good'. The horns of such dilemmas will typically be moral dualities, such as transparency and privacy, competition and cooperation, honesty and diplomacy, and courage and safety.

Which is the more ethically conscientious organization? The firm that states its values and enforces them? Or the firm that recognizes moral dilemmas and debates them?

For a value statement to be genuinely beneficial and not truistic ('do the right thing') or imprecise ('act with integrity'), it would need to acknowledge the **pluralistic** nature of morality and to make greater efforts towards helping executives notice, debate and resolve dilemmas as they arise within the firm.

Making it personal

London Business School, for whom three of us work, aims 'to have a profound impact on the way the world does business, and the way business impacts the world'. This, like other mission statements, may be sincere and well intentioned, but the question remains: is it likely that our behaviour will be shaped by these lofty values, written by someone else in the school but on our behalf and for our adherence? Or is each one of us sufficiently secure in – and clear about – our own personal code of ethics, not to want or need others to advocate the moral code by which we live?

Are your company values the self-chosen standard against which you invite others to judge you or are they moral duties to which any business person has a duty to submit?

How do **you,** in your own organization, respond to these kinds of moral entreaties? With sarcasm or respect? With weariness or excitement? With obedience or resistance?

Your response will depend, we expect, upon the motives that you attribute to those formulating these values statements. For example, returning to the investment bank's statement of 'core values' in its foyer, what purpose might the bankers themselves have had in mind?

1 An ideal to live up to and a standard against which to be judged?

2 An everyday reminder to staff of what is expected of them?

3 A competitive statement of strategic intent?

4 A confession or an apology for past transgressions, particularly as one of the prime movers of the 2008 financial crisis?

5 A boast or a reprimand to those accusing it of past misdemeanours?

6 A mix of all of these?

In defence of values statements

The conventional wisdom is that company values matter. Every conscientious firm is meant to have a set of norms to help its employees achieve not only their personal goals but also their shared objectives. They define the company's character and, if combined with a mission statement, encapsulate the purpose that it is seeking to serve.

Four kinds of rationale, all finding support in philosophical theory, have been used to support the practice of drawing up a set of values:

1 They establish the **frame** within which the members of the organization are free to behave as they wish. There is a link here with the concept of negative liberty, namely the idea that genuine liberty is freedom from interference by other people. Isaiah Berlin writes: 'Liberty in the negative sense involves an answer to the question, "What is the area within which the subject – a person or group of persons – is or should be left to do or be what he is able to do or be, without interference by other persons?"'[1] A statement of values defines the boundary between liberty and constraint.

2 They codify the **social contract** that binds the members of an organization together in the interests of the whole, forming the foundation necessary for any society, community or company to thrive. Rousseau argued that a citizen cannot pursue his true interest by being an egoist but must instead subordinate himself to the laws and values created by the citizenry acting as a collective. He expressed it this way: 'Each of us puts his person and all his power in common under the supreme direction of the general will; and in a body we receive each member as an indivisible part of the whole.'[2] A statement of values captures the general will.

3 They constitute the **norms** to which everyone signs up. They specify an ideal, or a model of perfection, that acts as a moral inspiration to everyone within the collective. The archetypal moral prescription is, of course, Kant's categorical imperative: 'Act only according to that maxim whereby you can, at the same time, will that it should become a universal law.'[3] It sets a standard. It assumes that, by an act of will, all of us are capable of meeting it.

4 They **signal** to the world at large the standards against which they invite others to judge them.

Choosing values as though from a menu

It is a rare company today that does not boast a statement of values, as though every business needed its equivalent of the Hippocratic oath in medicine. Yet, 50 years ago, this would have been a rare phenomenon. The great family firms of the 19th and early 20th centuries, most notably the formidable companies that had Quaker origins, such as Cadbury, Rowntree, Clarks, Barclays Bank, and Friends Provident, thrived without any need for an explicit set of principles. They simply lived their faith.

So why the sudden urge to proclaim the moral code by which everyone in the company is expected to comply? Could it be because standards have fallen, and with them, the performance of the firm? Or could it simply be a symptom of moral progress more generally whereby executives attend more carefully to the ethical manner in which performance is achieved?

The paradox, of course, is that for all the corporate talk about values, organizational behaviour is no more moral now than it was before the fashion for talking about it took hold. 'Walking the talk' remains as problematic as it ever was. Indeed, there may well be an inverse relationship between the amount of time we spend talking about morality and the amount of effort we invest in behaving morally. Ralph Waldo Emerson observed of an acquaintance: 'The louder he talked of his honour, the faster we counted our spoons'.[4]

With the crafting of values statements has come a subtle shift in the use of the word 'value'. Traditionally, 'value' was used as a singular noun standing for the worth or utility of something. For example, people would speak of the value of certain forms of behaviour, such as cooperation or reciprocity or courage, or of certain classes of assets, such as companies and properties. But now it has become a plural noun. We ascribe 'values' to individuals and organizations as a way of summarizing their beliefs, attitudes and dispositions. *My* values are contrasted with *yours*. Company A's values are set against Company B's. We are assumed to choose our values rather as we choose our clothes. There is a market in values: we choose the ones by which we want to live. We give ourselves the right to set the terms on which our virtue is to be judged. In other words, values have been marketized, monetized, personalized and relativized. The moral moorings that value once possessed in the more absolute world of virtue have been lost.

> There is a tendency for values to be at the service of strategy rather than strategy to be subject to morality. We treat values as ingredients in the competitive mix rather than strategy as choices constrained by moral considerations.

When a firm selects its values, it is making as strategic a choice as when it selects which markets to enter or which products to launch. With little reference to absolute standards or traditional morality, we construct our own subjective realm of personal and organizational ethics. The only test is its efficacy. If it advances our cause, then presumably our values have been skilfully chosen, and vice versa. In effect, ethical positioning has become an element of a company's competitive strategy and marketing mix.

In earlier times, virtue was not seen as a choice from a menu of options but as a hard-won habit. In his ethical writings, Aristotle observed that 'It is by doing just acts that the just man is produced, and by doing temperate acts the temperate man; without doing these no one would have even a prospect of becoming good.'[5]

This is what made the virtuous life rare, precious and praiseworthy. Virtues were practices acquired through diligence and humility. They were not lifestyle preferences or passing fads or means to an end. They were more akin to dispositions.

The distinction that we draw between values and virtue is akin to that between personality and character. Just as we would be embarrassed to use the word 'virtue' nowadays because of its sanctimonious overtones, so we find the word 'character' an anachronism in the assessment of a person. We may feel comfortable assessing a person's skills and personality, especially if couched in the pseudo-scientific language of competency profiling, but we feel less at ease assessing their virtue or their character. Yet corporate performance almost certainly depends more on virtue than values, and more on character than personality.

As George Will, an American journalist, recently remarked:

> The de-moralization of society is advanced when the word 'values' supplants the word 'virtues' in political and ethical contexts. When we move beyond talk of good and evil, when the categories virtue and vice are transcended, we are left with the thin gruel of values-talk.[6]

The source of moral complexity

At the height of the Second World War, a senior civil servant informed the secretaries in his department that he was about to commit a terrible thing. He was going to sack them all, despite knowing that only one of them was guilty of a grave offence. A leak of sensitive information to the enemy had been uncovered; someone in the office was guilty. Every effort to identify the culprit had failed. As a result, fighting men and women were meanwhile going to their deaths and Britain's war effort was being weakened. Faced with this situation, the official confessed, he had opted to fire the entire team so as to rule out the possibility of any further leaks. He acknowledged that this was a calamitous decision. None of those who were dismissed would ever again work in government, and there would be a shadow over their lives thereafter. Nevertheless, he concluded, it was the right thing to do.

Pluralism is the claim that moral dilemmas such as this confront us not as a choice between good and evil but between seemingly incompatible versions of what is right. It involves, in some sense, weighing one virtue against another. There is no single model of the good life – one that is best for all human beings, or indeed for any one of them. Christian humility, Buddhist detachment, Homeric valour, Aristotelian moderation, Kantian duty and Machiavellian cunning are all equally valid versions of the moral life. There is no vantage point from which they can be compared and judged.

The most vociferous and articulate advocate of this philosophy was Isaiah Berlin. Berlin was familiar with the case of the civil servant firing his team of secretaries during the war – and it influenced him deeply. He believed that what the official had done was right. But he also believed that, in this case, there were other ethically defensible choices that could have been made, such as doing nothing. Moral dilemmas arise as soon as one recognizes that, whatever choice one makes, a grave injustice is done. Often in life, and particularly in the pressurized conditions of the workplace, doing the right thing entails doing a lamentable wrong or inflicting irreparable harm.

To deny this fundamental aspect of human decision making was, in Berlin's eyes, to drain life of its complexity, mystery and variety. It depicted morality as an emaciated form of rule-following behaviour. He felt strongly that when the moral theories of philosophers conflict with the moral experience of mankind, we should jettison the theory.

He distrusted any kind of theodicy – the idea that morality, correctly understood, constitutes a harmonious whole.

In the same vein, Berlin objected to the Enlightenment ideal – the view that human reason would ultimately dismantle all the barriers that divide mankind and usher in a single harmonious civilization – not because it is impractical but because it is incoherent. He was repelled by the belief that there are historical laws of human progress, having known from personal experience as a child witnessing first-hand the Russian Revolution, how easily men are bewitched by utopian theories of inevitable progress. He pointed out that more human lives may have been sacrificed in the pursuit of this Enlightenment ideal than of any other human cause in history.

When we idolize a particular end state and proclaim all resistance to it as irrational or biased, terrible things are likely to ensue:

> What turns one inside out, and is indescribable, is the spectacle of one set of persons who so tamper and 'get at' others that the others do their will without knowing what they are doing; and in this lose their status as free human beings, indeed as human beings at all.[7]

Objective pluralism

Berlin believed that any mature code of ethics will create for its adherents moral dilemmas that reason alone cannot resolve, and that the values and ideals propounded by a complex morality such as our own will inevitably be plural and incommensurate. He thought that the idea of perfection, a state in which all values can be combined harmoniously, was incoherent.

Incommensurability does not imply indifference. As Joseph Raz, a philosophical contemporary of Berlin, has remarked, 'Incomparability does not ensure equality of merit or demerit. It does not mean indifference. It marks the inability of reason to guide our action, not the insignificance of our choice.'[8]

Berlin makes three claims on behalf of pluralism and against monism:

First, all moral codes, both historically and geographically, contain conflicting values. In a modern liberal society, for example, the values of liberty and equality, or fairness and welfare, or justice and mercy are at odds with one another. There is no 'higher value' that can be drawn upon to arbitrate the conflict between them.

Second, any one of these values itself contains internal inconsistencies. Both liberty and equality, for example, come in many guises, not all them mutually compatible. Liberty of information conflicts with liberty of privacy; and equality of opportunity clashes with equality of outcome.

Third, those moral codes that are embedded in particular cultures and civilizations each exemplify a particular way of life that has its own integrity, one that is sufficiently distinctive not to be easily combinable with any other.

Thus, value pluralism maintains that our deepest values are objective but irreducibly diverse. The implication for business is that the idea of a perfect organization in which all genuine ideals are achieved is not merely utopian or impractical, it is incoherent. Corporate life, like any individual life, teems with radical choices between ultimate ends, where reason leaves us in the lurch and whatever we do involves loss or harm.

So, in these circumstances, what is to be done? How do we lead in a morally pluralist world?

Pluralism in practice

Let us turn to a company that, for half a century, has recognized the plurality of values and seeks to be true to two seemingly opposed codes of conduct.

L'Oréal, the French cosmetics company, has long been inspired by a credo, first articulated by François Dalle, its president between 1957 and 1984: 'À la fois poète et paysan'… to be a poet and a peasant simultaneously. Dalle's visionary notion was that success for

L'Oréal would always reside in its ability to combine the virtues of creativity and common sense. For him, being a creative poet meant seeing the world anew, placing importance on beauty, coming up with ideas, giving oneself the chance to dream, to try out new solutions… whereas being the down-to-earth peasant meant being sensible, counting the pennies, trusting in tradition, keepings things simple, not getting above oneself….

It is the brave attempt to combine these two sets of seemingly contradictory values that partly explains L'Oréal's extraordinary success. So conscientiously do they keep faith with their credo that, to this day, they encourage a continuing dialogue between the poets and the peasants within the firm. They have 'confrontation rooms' set aside explicitly for these debates and discussions to take place and arrive at some kind of resolution. For example, all recruitment decisions are tested for their compatibility with their credo. They believe that it is only by conversing, arguing and learning from each other that both horns of the dilemma can be honoured – and the duality in some sense reconciled.

This aspect of L'Oréal's culture finds parallels in a particular initiative, launched by Jack Welch when CEO of General Electric, called 'Work-out' and designed to simplify operations by removing needless work. As a practice, it still flourishes within the organization. 'Work-out' is a structured method for encouraging operatives to come together to solve design issues normally reserved for management. In this sense, it was GE's way of giving 'poetic voice' to the 'peasant' or, in Welch's own words: 'Trust the people in the organization: the people in the best position to improve a business are the people in the job every day.'[9]

Work-out was powerful because it engaged the creativity of those who most intimately knew what needed to be re-engineered. Even though they 'lived' it every day, they had never before been asked to contribute their ideas. Like the confrontations in L'Oréal, the format consisted in fierce, no-holds-barred debates amongst everyone with skin in the game.

Most firms are fearful of open and robust debate. L'Oréal-style confrontations would be regarded as unhelpful, uncooperative, or even disloyal. As a result, truth takes second place to diplomacy. Differences of opinion are not surfaced and worked through. And yet, if most business problems entail the resolution of dilemmas, then open debate is essential. Karl Popper defined a good debate as one in which both sides sought not only to fully understand each other's arguments but also to strengthen their opponents' case before arguing the merits of their own case. This draws upon the skill of 'de-centring' and the emotional intelligence to see the world through the eyes of others as a prelude to building your own argument.

Moral dilemmas and the middle way

One way of describing a firm's strategic state of play is to identify the dilemmas that it is finding particularly troublesome. Typically, these might include:

- balancing the short and long term;
- weighing the economies of scale against those of simplicity and speed;
- privileging the interests of shareholders or a broader group of stakeholders;
- prioritizing the interests of customers or employees;
- operating as a hierarchy or as a network;
- emphasizing change or continuity;
- focusing upon functional excellence or inter-functional coordination.

When he was the CEO of ABB, Percy Barnevik echoed the challenges facing many large companies when declaring: 'We want to be global and local, big and small, radically decentralized with central reporting and control. If we can resolve those contradictions we can create real organizational advantage.'[10]

Barnevik had an instinctive feel for pluralism and the dualities that confront the leader. He knew, for example, that decentralization, as one policy option amongst many, offers both advantages and dangers. For example, it has the beneficial effect of releasing entrepreneurial energy in the organization, but simultaneously runs the risk of fragmentation, as opportunities for synergy and cross-boundary cooperation are neglected.

Addressing dilemmas

All dilemmas pose this seemingly irresolvable problem: how to combine the strengths of both extremes without incurring the weakness of either. This is not easy. What happens in practice is that we tend to fudge the issue:

- We procrastinate: we muddle along, pretending that there is no dilemma and that therefore there is no fundamental choice to be made – the tactic of **indecision.**

- We arbitrarily cast our lot in favour of one horn of the dilemma rather than the other; we use the pretext that 'this is how we do things around here' and we harden it into an aspect of our corporate culture – the tactic of **polarization.**

- We oscillate between one extreme and another; we swing back and forth as the mood takes us, or as fashion dictates, or as periodic crises panic us into doing – the tactic of a **pendulum.**

- We try to anticipate the point at which one extreme needs to give way to the other, running the risk of making the call too early ('panicking prematurely') or too late ('missing the boat') – the tactic of **foresight.**

- We seek the middle way, trading one extreme off against the other – the tactic of **compromise.**

Every firm has its behavioural biases, often rooted in its history or in the experiences of its leaders. Based upon the fortuitous nature of success, most leaders know only one 'trick' – the policy to which they credit their success and the mindset that got them to where they are. This could be cost control, kaizen, total quality management, outsourcing, acquisitions, financial incentives, lean manufacturing, or any other managerial 'panacea'. Wherever they go and whatever the situation, they take with them their all-purpose remedy – the magic recipe that has never failed them.

Sometimes, the recipe hardens into a managerial slogan, such as shareholder value, or customer-centricity, or corporate social responsibility. At other times, the recipe is described as the 'core competence' of the corporation. The key point is that it tends to become a fixation that leads in turn to a stall-point in performance. This is an instance of the 'failure of success', sometimes called 'the Icarus phenomenon'. Hubris entices the heroic leader to overplay his hand, to push his luck too far, and to turn a blind eye to any countervailing evidence.

It is a rare leader who can spot the moment when the trick or the slogan becomes inappropriate. The more precarious the situation, the likelier it will be that leaders hunker down, stay close to what they know, and emphasize group loyalty and solidarity. Only when the situation becomes so dire that the spell is broken does a radical change of direction become the only option. The danger then is that the new leadership simply puts in place the same pathology *but in reverse*. And so the cycle continues. Indeed, cyclical performance is the classic symptom of the firm that has over-extended its faith in a simplistic solution that does not squarely address the original dilemma.

In classical Greek, the meaning of 'di-lemma' was 'two propositions'. Today, we speak of being stuck on the horns of a dilemma. We recognize the situation whenever we have a difficult decision to make. If we give undue preference to one horn of the dilemma, we are likely to be impaled by the horn that we neglected.

The assumption on which we typically try to resolve these dilemmas is that the choice we have to make is **between** the 'values-in-tension'. In other words, we need to **take sides**. But might there be an alternative way of handling dilemmas, one that does justice to both horns? Instead of arbitrating between one horn and another, or ranking one arbitrarily above the other, might we be able to combine their virtues, or reconcile them in some way?

A workplace that is fulfilling is one that acknowledges the daily reality of moral dilemmas in organizational life and treats each person as a stakeholder in the resolution of these dilemmas.

The method of reconciliation

The test of a first-rate intelligence is the ability to hold two opposed ideas in the mind at the same time, and still retain the ability to function.

F SCOTT FITZGERALD[11]

What does it mean to manage in a pluralistic world? For example, in managing a clash of values, what rational method can we call upon? One answer, suggested by Charles Hampden-Turner, a British management philosopher and senior research associate at the Judge Business School, is to treat each polarity as an opportunity for finding a place of reconciliation.

To take an example, how might the virtues of bureaucracy, such as order and control, be reconciled with the virtues of innovation, such as dynamism and learning? Bureaucracy runs the risk of being stuck and stultifying, whilst learning is often too chaotic and undisciplined for its own good. Learning relies upon trial and error, whereas bureaucracy thrives on 'right first time'. So how can the values of control and learning be combined in a way that enhances the practice of both?

The idea of reconciliation – as opposed to compromise – is that we borrow the virtues of one to improve the practice of the other. To pursue the example, we become more controlled and disciplined in the way that we learn, and we become more open minded and exploratory in the way that we exercise control.

For example, we could invite the accountants in the firm to find a way of measuring the pace of organizational learning relative to our competitors, and put our R&D scientists on to the task of re-inventing the metrics of organizational risk. The idea is to combine, in new ways, order and playfulness, or rationality and creativity, or predictability and discovery. In short, we practise the virtues of experimentation.

The oblique principle is relevant here. When **A** and **B** are seemingly conflicting values, being true to **A** may best be achieved by asking how **B** can strengthen **A**, *and vice versa.*

We 'triangulate' the polarity.

A particularly sticky dilemma faced by many corporations is the contentious issue of how executives should be financially incentivized and rewarded. For example, should bonuses be paid for personal achievement or team achievement? Should everyone share equally in the success of the firm as a whole or should rewards differentiate between high-performing and low-performing individuals and units?

In most firms nowadays, there is an arbitrary balance struck between the proportion of someone's bonus that is paid for collective achievement and the proportion for personal achievement; say, 70 per cent based on the firm's performance and 30 per cent on that of the individual. This 'two bucket' approach to a bonus plan suggests that these two definitions of performance – collective and individual – are somehow independent of one another, as though the firm's performance is unrelated to the efforts of those who work for it.

Advanced Micro Devices (AMD), a multinational semiconductor company based in California, has pioneered a way of rewarding its employees that reconciles personal achievement and team contribution. Individuals are rewarded for their contribution to the teams of which they are a member, *as judged by the teams themselves*; and the teams are rewarded for their ability to draw upon the talents of the individuals who work for them, *as judged by the individuals themselves*. This is an example of a masterly synthesis of seemingly opposing values.

Early in his career, when he was running the plastics division in GE, Jack Welch recognized the pervasive character of dilemmas in the workplace and the importance of reconciling what appear to be opposing values. These are some of the maxims by which he ran the business:

- practise planful opportunism;
- wallow in information until you find the simple solution;

- test ideas through constructive conflict;
- treat all subordinates as equals, but reward each one strictly according to merit.

Paul Evans, a professor of human resource management, has sought to generalize the skill of managing in a pluralistic world by putting forward the following principle:

Organize one way, but the manage the other.[12]

He recognized that most companies are organized along lines that favour certain values, typically control, alignment and predictability. Given that these values are built into the corporate culture, but that other, equally important values are not, the role of management should be to ensure that the latter values, such as curiosity, exploration, diversity and trust find their due weight. The role of the leader, in other words, is to focus on the 'neglected polarity'. If the organization happens to be wired to serve the shareholder, then management would be wise to emphasize the customer and how this enhances shareholder value. It is the same with other dualities, such as cost and revenue, or stability and growth, or analysis and action.

To summarize, management is as much a matter of resolving dilemmas as solving problems.

Conclusions

Most value statements operate on the tacit assumption that employees need to be reminded of the moral criteria against which their decisions are made and the moral standards by which their behaviour is judged.

It may well be important that, as leaders, we keep reminding ourselves of what counts as virtue. But the moral issues that are troublesome in business today typically take the form of dilemmas, where different virtues compete for our allegiance, and where, therefore, lists of values and books of rules are insufficient to the task of balancing one virtue against another, determining 'the exchange rate' between them and discovering some degree of reconciliation.

Instead of spending time defining values statements we need to focus on the management of dilemmas, through moral curiosity and dialogue. We need to encourage discussion, dissent and debate, with the result that moral behaviour moves beyond mere compliance to conscientious inquiry. And an ethically serious organization is one that is alert to moral issues and addresses them directly and openly.

Morality in business becomes more like a creative project and an unfinished quest than a jigsaw puzzle or a rule book.

Questions

1 What do the decisions you make tell others about your values?

2 How can you explain the moral dilemmas inherent in your decisions when communicating your decisions?

3 What guidance would you give to your teams to help them surface and work with the moral dilemmas in their decision making, to encourage discussion and dissent?

To debate and to dissent is to believe that what you think and what you do matters, that it is important that you strive to do the right thing. We have seen that values do not tell us the right thing, they provide guidance and in so doing present us with dilemmas. The final chapter confronts us with the ultimate leadership challenge – to use the freedom we have to do what we believe is the right thing to do.

Notes

1 Berlin, I (1958) Two Concepts of Liberty, reprinted in *Four Essays on Liberty*, Oxford University Press, 1969

2 Rousseau, J J (1762) *The Social Contract*, Book I, Chapter VI

3 Kant, I (1785) *Groundwork of the Metaphysics of Morals*

4 Emerson, R W (1860) *Conduct of Life: A Philosophical Reading*

5 Aristotle, *The Nicomachean Ethics*, Book II

6 Will, G (2000) Forget values, let's talk virtues, *Jewish World Review*, 25 May

7 Letter to George Kennan (13 February 1951), in *Isaiah Berlin, Enlightening: Letters 1946–1960*, ed Henry Hardy and Jennifer Holmes, Chatto and Windus, London, 2012

8 Raz, J (1986) *The Morality of Freedom*, Oxford University Press, p. 333

9 Quoted in Golding, I (2017) Engaging your people in improvement activity: 6 key questions, *Customer Think*, 16 February

10 Quoted in Magwood, J (2011) Global Socio-Cultural Expectations on Ethics, *Customer Think*, 3 September

11 Fitzgerald, F S (1936) The crack up, *Esquire Magazine*

12 Paul Evans, personal communication

10

The freedom to do what you can

In this chapter, with the help of 20th-century philosophers Peter Strawson and Jean-Paul Sartre, and ancient Greek philosopher Socrates, we learn about ourselves as individuals with our own agency, our own ideas of what is right and wrong, and the difference we want to make to the world – our leadership. Whatever our level of seniority, authority or command of resources, the question is how we use the freedom we have to lead – to make a positive difference – to flourish. Once again our ideas about empowerment are central to the pursuit of flourishing. To be empowered we need to understand and act in accordance with the freedoms we have, the freedom to strive to do what we believe is right despite the constraints we face.

We started Chapter 6 with the story of our experience following an inclusion and diversity conference for a European organization. The story goes as follows:

> A few months ago, the authors were invited to give a keynote speech and run a workshop at a diversity and inclusion day for a client in Europe. The session was well attended by middle managers and staff. Everyone participated enthusiastically, and at the end of the workshop several participants spoke to us. Their message was clear and simple: 'You have to tell senior management that we feel completely excluded and *un-empowered*, boxed in by rules and regulations with no *authority* or *freedom* to make decisions'.

We explored the response from senior management and proposed that **instead of merely focusing on including the views of managers and staff in their decision making, senior managers should focus on creating an environment in which empowered people will flourish.** We examined the purpose and legitimacy of authority in organizations and concluded that we have too often, in the post-Kantian world, got it upside down. **We should recognize that authority is delegated upward not downwards and that our duty is to exercise what authority we have justly, for the benefit of others.**

Be careful what you wish for

But what about those who seek to be empowered? The managers and staff who feel boxed in, excluded, ignored and un-empowered. What is their responsibility in the empowerment, authority and freedom challenge? What is their leadership challenge?

The main question that we hear repeatedly from our CEO clients is, 'How can I create an organization that is more innovative, adaptable, agile and sustainable?' The answer they get from many of their consultant advisers is, 'You need to empower your people'. The problem is, as we discussed in Chapter 6, the all-too-common 'empowerment' programme is based on the myth that senior people can empower others; the truth is that empowerment is a quality of the individual, not a gift bestowed on others by those with hierarchical power. People with more seniority in the hierarchy should use their authority to support those seeking to exercise their freedom and deploy their power to make good things happen. This is not the same as saying that senior people can empower others. They cannot.

If we accept the combined thinking of Hobbes and Kant, as explored in Chapter 6, with respect to our inherent equality, our power for self-governance and our innate sense of duty, then we are all capable of being empowered – making decisions and taking action based on what we think is the right thing to do.

Working out what you think needs to be done and making the decision to make it happen is an empowered way of being and an act of leadership. Doing so has many consequences. On the positive side we gain a sense of purpose, feel we are making a contribution, that what we do counts, and our self-esteem rises as does the esteem in which we are held – our honour is upheld. But there are risks. By acting, making decisions, making stuff happen, we take responsibility and with responsibility comes worry. What if it goes wrong? What if I upset someone? What if the amount of effort and energy required to persist is beyond me? Worse still, we have to contemplate all these risks without the certainty of success. Perhaps it would be easier to follow convention, or to ask for permission, or wait to be asked, or simply follow the guidelines or someone else's instructions?

> We all face this dilemma in taking responsibility: whether to take the initiative and exercise our freedom to act, or to take the easier way out. It is how we face the dilemma that determines the extent to which we are empowered; the extent to which we lead.

What can philosophers teach us about our freedom to act and our responsibility as leaders?

You'll notice that above we've used the phrase 'exercise our freedom to act'. It's important for us to be clear what we mean by our freedom to act. Among philosophers, there is much discussion about the existence of free will. Hardline determinists argue against the existence of free will and hardline 'free willers' (libertarians) argue for the existence of free will. The hardline determinists believe that all our actions are caused by previous events or natural laws of nature and that the idea that we are making free choices is a delusion. The hardline 'free willers' believe that we have genuine choice over what we do and the choice we make is not predetermined by outside forces. One argument that tries to find a middle way between those that believe there is no free will and everything is predetermined and those who believe we are free to make non-predetermined choices with different consequences, is known as compatibilism. This is the approach taken by the philosopher Peter Strawson (1919–2006) and explored in his 1962 essay *Freedom and Resentment*.[1]

Strawson came into the world just as the First World War ended and lived through the devastation of the Second World War and the subsequent battle for ideological supremacy between capitalism and communism, played out through the Cold War. This was a time, due to the cock-ups, brutality, and bloody-minded stupidity of some of those in authority, that the respect and deference so many 'leaders' had taken for granted at the beginning of the 20th century was no longer readily forthcoming. Following the horrors of the Second World War, where the fight for freedom, the anger of alienation and the quest for domination culminated in a global bloodbath, it is not surprising that many philosophers and others focused their attention on the nature of freedom, including the existentialist school, which we will encounter through the thinking of Jean-Paul Sartre later in the chapter.

The incident of the cat and the wheelie bin

Strawson reasons that we all behave as if free will existed, and this is nowhere more apparent than when we are considering handing out blame and punishment. He argues we acknowledge circumstances in which people can be excused from their actions. We have phrases like 'she was not in her right mind' and 'he was not himself', and we take account of mental illness as a mitigating condition explaining or excusing certain negative behaviour. In other words, we suspend our normal responses to the acts of others when we consider them not to be in charge of themselves to the extent that most of us are considered to be most of the time.

To put it simply, if I'm of sound mind and decide to pick up a neighbour's cat and deposit it in a wheelie bin in the hope that it will be taken away by the refuse collectors and never plague my peace of mind again, and if, say, I was caught on CCTV in the act of so doing, I would be considered, by most people of sound mind, as worthy of reprimand for choosing such a callous act. On the other hand, if I were to argue, perhaps with the support of the medical profession, that the stress of not sleeping for weeks due to the caterwauling of said cat has driven me out of my mind with despair, then some people of sound mind may feel I should be given a break and be allowed to go free without reprimand.

This is Strawson's argument: we suspend normal reactions when we talk about an individual as not being themselves, ie not acting freely but compelled in some way to do what they did by dint of not being themselves – and consequently hand out fewer or no punitive consequences – versus when we consider there to be no compulsion or mitigating circumstances and more severe consequences are meted out, ie we hold an individual to account for their actions. This gives rise to the definition of freedom as being the absence of compulsion or mitigating circumstances. In other words, when there is no choice to be made, people are not responsible and do not have free will, but where there is, they do. This idea of freedom is fundamental to the idea of empowerment and leadership. Assuming, of course, we are of sound mind.

> Freedom is not the ability to act without consequences. Freedom is the ability to choose to act without compulsion and face the consequences, some, if not most of which may be unknown at the point of decision. This is acting as a leader.

Even if organizations were prisons

This is not to say that others don't have authority over you, however senior or junior you may be, and may act to stop you or even punish you for your actions. If we are part of Kant's 'Kingdom of Ends', as discussed in Chapter 6 – a world in which we both shape and accept communal rules by which we will live – we have by definition signed up to the fact that some of our actions will be constrained and we may even be reprimanded if we break certain rules. We have accepted the idea that others, who with our permission have authority over us, may impose penalties on us, for example, if we should fail to pay our taxes. All societies have a justice system comprising rules, judges and consequences for breaking the rules. But even in extreme cases such as prison, the principle still applies that you have a choice. We can think of no better example than when Nelson Mandela, who was offered freedom in 1985 on the condition that he take no further part in political life, chose to stay in prison. He was eventually released five years later with no strings attached. That is the act of an empowered person.

For most of us, the circumstances in which we have to decide what to do, what we stand for, what difference we make, do not determine the length of our time incarcerated. But these questions are a very real part of life and apply to all of us.

The questions, what do I stand for and what difference do I make, have been with us since time immemorial and like all such age-old questions have attracted the attention of philosophers.

Socrates – by force of spiritedness

In the *Republic*,[2] Plato (427–347 BC), reported the words of Socrates (470–399 BC), exploring the 'what difference do I make' question through the idea of spiritedness (thymos). Socrates describes the soul as comprising three parts: reason (rational thinking), desire (appetite) and spiritedness. He defined spiritedness as our sense of honour.

Socrates himself embodied spiritedness. He lived in a time in which Athenian dominance was in decline in the face of Spartan ambition. His outspoken questioning of the Athenian government led to him being put on trial, where he was found guilty and sentenced to death by poisoning. His friends tried to persuade him to escape as they had the means to get him out of prison, but he refused. His arguments for remaining in prison and facing his fate revolved around his principles and determination to do the honourable thing, the right thing. He argued he should obey the laws of the society he had elected to be part of by moving to Athens. He knew the laws and they were applied with due procedure. That is spiritedness. Spiritedness is our ability to be driven by our passions. Our passions, of course, can move us to do great things or terrible things.

We see another example of spiritedness in revisiting Nelson Mandela's act in declining to be released from prison. By force of reason alone it makes sense to take the offer to be released. Why? There are many reasons: it may not ever be offered again. Does it matter if I, Nelson Mandela, retreat from the political struggle? Have I not done enough? There are others who can take up the fight. By force of desire alone the offer is compelling. How? Because to walk freely again and enjoy all that life has to offer, that has been denied for so long, to satisfy one's appetites, is an overwhelming force to accept the offer of release. Yet by force of spiritedness the offer is declined. What Mandela would have gained by accepting the offer would have been a more comfortable life that many people would reason he deserved. What would have been lost was everything he stood for, his honour.

An examination of the power of thymos, spiritedness – to override the force of self-interest and desire – quickly reveals that spiritedness is more than bloody-mindedness. It asks questions. What am I about beyond what self-interest would compel any person to do? What am I about beyond what desire could seduce any person to do? What do I believe I should do? And why is that so powerful? Because to fail to do what I believe I should do is to face myself and ask what I stand for and why it matters what I do. It is a matter of the value I ascribe to myself. It is a matter of my honour. It is a failure of leadership. It also asks the question, 'How in the gaze of others will I be seen?' Anyone (and that includes all of us) caught in the act of unseemly behaviour, or failure to do the right thing, by one whose approving gaze we seek, knows only too well the gut-wrenching pain of losing the esteem of others. Which brings us back to Plato, who argued through Socrates that spiritedness is the source of indignation and self-anger or shame. These emotions are a reaction to an attack on our sense of self-worth.

> Empowerment is the ability to act without compulsion, without certainty of the consequences, in a way that you can answer the question, 'Was I able to do what I believe I should do?' with a 'Yes'.

No more sweeteners

Savio Kwan, ex-COO and president of Alibaba, was one of the first executives to join Jack Ma when Alibaba employed 150 people and was struggling in its early days as an internet start-up and facing disaster. During his time at Alibaba, Kwan saw the company become one of the world's biggest B2B companies with over 2,500 staff generating over US $5 million surplus cash per month.

Earlier in his career, Savio was appointed by General Electric to head business development for the GE Medical Systems business in Asia. At the time there was a culture in the client base of expecting 'sweeteners' in order to give the deal to the supplier. GE's company policy with regards to giving and/or taking bribes, based on the US Government's Foreign Corrupt Practices Act (FCPA), was no bribes – ever! The problem was not that the GE medical team in China did not know the policy, but that 'no one would bring this up with our customers for fear of offending them due to cultural sensitivities'.

For Savio, brought up in a fusion of the teachings of both the Catholic Church and Confucius, this had to be confronted. From the point of view of duty of care for his staff he had to act to protect them – any violation by any GE employees would lead to dismissal and even the possibility of prison sentences. From the point of view of the business and wasting time chasing deals that eventually would not be signed off by GE – any deal with a sweetener would not be signed off – he had to safeguard the proper and effective use of company resources. And from his own ethical standpoint he had to 'confront the "beast" upfront rather than staying under the shadow of cultural nicety':

I started training everyone on the need to come out from the shadow of nicety and to shout from the tree tops on GE's position regarding this, right from the first meeting with the customers in China. The team all thought I had gone crazy but there was method to the seeming madness as this was our first step in 'Qualifying our customers', ie those who would need a bribe of any sort were not our target customers as GE's policy on no bribing (called policy 20.4) would mean no deal under any circumstances, so why waste your time following something that would not be allowed in any case?

This simple action required the GE medical sales team in China to filter out all the deals that required a bribe (about 70 per cent at the time) and to focus on those that did not.

Through his innate spiritedness, his determination to do the right thing, Savio had to confront the problem head-on. His sales team reacted badly, telling him they would get nowhere by ignoring 70 per cent of the market. His response: 'Then we will capture the others and build our business from there.' As a result they captured 25 per cent of the market. 'There were many tough conversations that ensued, with customers who could not believe there would be no sweeteners.' But there were no sweeteners.

The empowered organization

In the introduction to the book we point out that while instrumental in the effectiveness and success of many of our organizations, reliance on economic and psychological thinking alone is not enough. Neither discipline sheds light on the ethical issues facing us as we seek to work together to lead fulfilling and meaningful lives, to flourish. Just as we cannot pretend hierarchy does not exist, we cannot pretend that differences in power and the distribution of resources do not exist. For an empowered person these differences are no excuse for the unethical use of authority or the unethical abdication of responsibility to do, within the realms of possibility, the right thing – to lead.

There is no simple rulebook for creating an empowered organization. It takes all of us to behave in ways that create the environment for others to flourish and to make choices to act in ways that we believe are right. Taking the arguments from the philosophers in this chapter and Chapter 6, if we believe that people are inherently equal, with the power of self-governance (as did Hobbes), that we have a duty to treat others as an end in themselves (as did Kant), that we have the freedom to make choices for better or for worse (as did Strawson) and that our sense of what is right can override our self-interest and desires (as did Socrates), then we must reflect on the philosophical questions: what does it mean to exercise authority justly? And, what does it take to act in accordance with what you believe is right? For an empowered person, a leader, these questions are always front of mind.

An exercise in self-empowerment

A colleague of ours, Robert Sadler, many years ago introduced us to a simple and powerful exercise to help anyone reconnect with their flourishing empowered self – to lead. The exercise is as follows.

- Go back in three-year time periods over your life and select for each period a time when you felt most fulfilled. This will be a time when you felt 'in the zone', time flew by, and you generally leapt out of bed in the morning keen to continue the work, project or whatever you were engaged in. Do this (if you are old enough) for five instances, ie go back over 15 years.

- Team up with two colleagues/friends and invite one person to interview you about each of these times in succession. The other person should observe and note what patterns emerge that are common elements of the times when you were flourishing.

- There are four questions (or variations of) that should be asked by the interviewer with respect to each occasion:

  ○ How did you get into this flourishing situation – did someone ask you? Did you initiate it? Was it forced upon you?

  ○ How did you learn what you needed to know and or be able to contribute?

○ What was it like? Were other people involved? Was it technically challenging? Was it fast paced? Was it breaking new ground? Was it...?

○ What was fulfilling about it? What was meaningful about it?

Once the interview has finished, the observer plays back what they have heard in terms of the patterns that describe the elements that create a flourishing environment for the person being interviewed. It is valuable, and only fair, to repeat the process for the other two participants with each person having a turn as interviewer, interviewee and observer. What emerges is a powerful combination of the ingredients that are common to us all in creating a flourishing environment and those ingredients that are specific to us as individuals. The common elements are expressions of:

· feeling that I am in control;

· feeling that I am making a positive difference;

· feeling I am valued;

· feeling that I am learning.

For each individual, of course, there will be a wide range of specific ingredients that are unique to that person. Those of us who expect others to create an environment in which we can flourish will have a long wait. Those of us who fear the consequences of making changes to our lives to create the environment in which we may flourish will have a long list of regrets.

> An empowered person, a leader, is someone who recognizes the common and specific ingredients that make for a flourishing life for them and acts to secure as many of these ingredients as possible, as often as possible. You cannot lead others unless you yourself are flourishing.

Bronnie Ware, a palliative nurse, lists in her book describing her discussion with terminally ill patients[3] the most common regrets of those in her care as they approached death. She lists the top five regrets as follows:

1 I wish I'd had the courage to live a life true to myself, not the life others expected of me;

2 I wish I hadn't worked so hard;

3 I wish I'd had the courage to express my feelings;

4 I wish I had stayed in touch with my friends;

5 I wish that I had let myself be happier.

In our work with executives from all over the world, we hear many of the warning bells of such regrets: 'I don't have time to think'; 'However hard I work I never seem to be able to get on top of things'; 'My boss demotivates me'; 'I can't afford to make a mistake'; 'I feel unempowered'. The central ingredient at the heart of these warning bells and regrets is the business of making choices. To say 'I wish I had…' is to imply that at the time I had a choice, and I chose what I now regret.

> To say you can never get on top of things is to accept that things are driving you and you have no choice, rather than you are driving things through your choices.

It is not uncommon for many of us in the moment of decision to claim that we have no choice. If I don't work hard I will be fired, or I won't get promoted; if I do what I want I will be seen as selfish. Sometimes, our sense of lack of choice is driven by fear – such as losing our job – and sometimes by an aspiration to live up to a value – to be seen as selfless, not selfish. However it is dressed up, the existentialist philosophers take a very dim view of this kind of excusing.

The existentialists come at life from a fundamentally different perspective than many that came before. The fundamental tenet of existential philosophy is that existence precedes essence; essence does not precede existence. What this means is that unlike Kant, who believed in the categorical imperative – we are hard-wired to do the right thing and that if we do not we suffer, ie there is an essence of a person that precedes his or her existence – the existentialist believes that no such blueprint of what it means to be human exists.

For Kant, his insistence that we treat people not merely as a means to an end but as an end in themselves is not open to negotiation, it is not hypothetical, it does not depend on circumstance. Consequently, for Kant, all of us come into existence with this essence of being a person central to our life. The essence is in the blueprint. This begs the question of course, who created the blueprint? In the case of philosophies based on Abrahamic religion the answer is God. The essence of humankind, for Christians or for Muslims, is determined by the Creator and our task is to flourish according to the blueprint that the essence constitutes. For the existentialist there is no such preordained essence that precedes existence. Neither is there support for Aristotle's views on living reasonably discussed much earlier in the book, which presuppose that theoretical reason can tell us how to live.

The question of whether there is or is not a God, or how reason guides our actions, is not the main concern of existentialists. There are Catholic existentialists and Atheist existentialists. Existentialism is very much a philosophy of the 20th century, and Jean-Paul Sartre (1905–80) is probably the most well-known of the Atheist existentialists. Sartre lived through the two 'Great Wars' of the 20th century, a devastating period during which the peoples of the world suffered catastrophically from the failure of the proclaimed honourable essence of humankind to protect them from atrocities inflicted by human upon human.

During the First World War, on one day, 1 July 1916, 54,000 British soldiers were killed or severely injured. During the Second World War, 26 million Russians died, including 8 million from famine and disease. As a result of Nazi population policy, 6 million Jews, 250,000 people with disabilities and 1.8 million non-Jewish Polish citizens died. In India, under British rule, 1 million people died of famine in 1900 and 2.1 million people died in 1944. There are many other examples of the utter failure of the established religious or secular authorities to uphold some semblance of a beneficent human essence during the 20th century. This is the context in which existentialism was born.

But existentialism – and Sartre in particular – is not a counsel of despair. In his relatively accessible lecture, *Existentialism Is a Humanism*, given in 1946,[4] Sartre set out the optimistic humanistic existentialist approach to human flourishing.

The idea is simple – you are what you choose to be. It is challenging – excuses are seen as forms of denial of responsibility – and it is optimistic – fundamentally based on the idea of freedom. As Sartre puts it: 'For at bottom, what is alarming in [existentialism] ... [is] that it confronts man with a possibility of choice.' And for those who fail to exercise their choice, there remains within them 'a wide range of abilities, inclinations and potentialities, unused but perfectly viable...'.

In his lecture, Sartre provides us with a philosophical precursor to the top five regrets listed by Bronnie Ware. It takes us back to our exercise in empowering ourselves, looking back over our lives and recognizing when we were flourishing, when we were leading – whether by example, by infectious enthusiasm, by making things happen or serving others – and demands a response: are we choosing to flourish or are we blaming others, circumstances or plain bad luck for our circumstances?

> Once you are aware of the conditions in which you are able to flourish as a human being, it is your choice, through your actions that decide whether you flourish or not, whether to lead or to comply, whether to take responsibility or to blame.

Sartre and the other existentialists talk about anguish and abandonment as fellow travellers on the path of a flourishing existence. Anguish because taking responsibility is to face the possibility of getting it wrong; abandonment because taking responsibility means throwing away the crutches provided by excuses or the direction of others. Anyone who acts without compulsion, without certainty of the consequences in a way that they can answer the question, 'Was I able to do what I believed I should do?' with a 'Yes', knows the anguish of so doing and the moment of loneliness (abandonment) of committing to the chosen course of action – to lead.

It is not easy to live an empowered, flourishing life, but it is the responsibility of each of us to endeavour to do so, to give voice to our spiritedness, to make our leadership contribution. It will mean confronting our fears, stepping out without certainty of the outcome, disappointing some, incurring the anger of others, feeling out of our depth – in other words, leading. The alternative is living a life of regret.

Summary

- We all face a dilemma in taking responsibility, ie whether to take the initiative and exercise our freedom to act despite the unknown consequences, or whether to take the easier way out. It is how we face this dilemma that determines the extent to which we are empowered; the extent to which we lead.

- Freedom is not the ability to act without consequences. Freedom is the ability to choose to act without compulsion and face the consequences, some or most of which may be unknown at the point of decision.

- Empowerment is the ability to act without compulsion, without certainty of the consequences in a way that you can answer the question, 'Was I able to do what I believed I should do?' with a 'Yes'.

- An empowered person is someone who recognizes the common and specific ingredients that make for a flourishing life for them and acts to secure as many of these ingredients as possible, as often as possible.

- Once you are aware of the conditions in which you are able to flourish as a human being, it is your choice – through your actions that decide whether you flourish or not – whether you lead.

So, what should we do? There is no formulaic answer. Instead there are key questions that, if we ask them and allow the answers to guide our behaviour, will help us make progress. We suggest some questions below; you may have better ones.

Questions

1 I am a person with authority: what can I do more of, less of, or start doing to create an environment in which empowered people can flourish?

2 I am a person trying to do my best within the constraints around me: what can I do to clarify for myself what I believe is right, and what should I stop doing, do more of and do less of to bring about what I believe is right?

3 I am a person who can flourish: what can I do to secure the conditions to enable me to flourish – to lead?

Notes

1 Strawson, P (2008) *Freedom and Resentment*, Routledge, Oxford
2 Plato, *The Republic,* Penguin Classics, 2007
3 Ware, B (2011) *The Top Five Regrets of the Dying: A life transformed by the dearly departing,* Hay House
4 Kaufman, W (ed) (1989) *Existentialism from Dostoyevsky to Sartre*, Meridian Publishing Company, Chapter 10, Part 4

INDEX

3E model 97
360-degree feedback 35, 117

abandonment 200–01
Ackoff, Russell 74
adaptability 108, 120
Advanced Micro Devices (AMD) 182
agreement 155
Alibaba 194
alienation 3–8, 13
all-purpose remedies 179–80
Amazon 4
Ambler, Tim 77
anguish 200–01
animal spirits 28–30
annual engagement surveys 143–46
anxiety 127–28
Apple 51
applications processing department
        problem 105
Apprenticeshop, The 39–40
Argentinian red wine 50–51, 59
Aristotle 9, 21–22, 25–30, 38–39, 41, 89, 173
ARM 51
asymmetric knowledge 62–64
attunement states 19
authority 191–92
    collapse of moral authority 32–33
    and empowerment 11, 101–22
    as a gift 11, 106–09, 110, 121
    Hobbes 11, 101, 103, 109, 110–13
    Kant 11, 101, 103, 109, 113–17
autonomous will 115, 189–90
Axial Age 48

Bacon, Francis 71
banking 52
    Barings Bank 27–28
    investment bank's values
        statement 166–67, 170
bargaining power 45–48
Barings Bank 27–28
Barnevik, Percy 178–79
being 159, 160
    and seeming 152, 155

Berkshire Hathaway 64
Berlin, Isaiah 12, 170, 174–76
biases 135–36
Black, Sir James 85
blunders, government 75–76
body–mind separation 161–62
bold conjectures 74, 75
bonuses 182
Bragg, Sir Lawrence 84
breakfast meetings 104
Buber, Martin 12, 143, 150–51, 152, 156
Buddha, Gautama 9–10, 48–53, 54–55, 56
Buffett, Warren 64–66, 70
business schools 1, 16–17
buy-in 18, 148–49
    see also engagement
buzzword bingo 43

capital markets 60–70
    asymmetric knowledge 62–64
    lessons from 70
    market inefficiency 64–65
    Soros and human fallibility 67–69
cascade of curated information 124–25
Casson, Mark 73
categorical imperative 114–18, 171, 198
    and leadership 115–18
category mistakes 66–67
Cavendish Laboratory 84–88, 92
centredness 162
change agents 124–25
change initiatives 124–28
character 173
chief ethical officers (CEOs) 118–20
China 4
    army 98
Christianity 31–32, 90
cognitive knowing 161–62
collaboration 50–53
colleague letters of understanding
        (CLOUs) 94–95
collective action 117
collusion 97–98
commitment to act 138–39
commoditization of people 7

common sense 176–77
communication 11–12, 123–42
    Haidt 123, 130, 134, 135–36, 137, 140
    Hume 11, 123, 130, 134, 138–39, 140
    sense-making 136–37, 139–40
    stoic philosophy 11, 131–34, 140
    'tell' approach 11, 123, 124–30, 132,
        151
    understanding 134–36
compatibilism 189–91
competitive advantage 44–48, 51
compromise 179
compulsion, acting without 190–91
confrontation rooms 177
conjectures, bold 74, 75
connectedness in action 50–53
contracts 112–13
    social contract 110–13, 171
control 133, 181
    dichotomy of 131–32, 134
    fallacy of 126–27, 132
cooperation 46–48
coordination 46–48
corporate governance 117
corporate incompetence 76–77
corporate value statements 166–73
courage 26
craft workers 3
creating space
    for others to flourish 104–06, 120
    where anything is possible 140–41
creativity 85, 176–77
    and critical thinking 10, 59–81
Crewe, Ivor 75–76
critical rationalism 71–72, 72–73
critical thinking 10, 59–81
Cuban Missile Crisis 52

Dalle, François 176–77
debate 177–78
decentralization 178–79
deductive falsification 71–72
dehumanized workplace 1–8
delegated authority 103, 107–08
    upwards delegation 103, 117–18, 121
deliberate strategy 55
delusion 49
demanding engagement 147
dependence 127–28
dependency 102
Descartes, René 161
desire 192–93
determinists 189
dialogue, fair process 96–97

dichotomy of control 131–32, 134
difference principle 91
dilemmas 168–69, 173–83, 183–84
    addressing 179–83
    middle way and 178–79
discontinuities, market 68
discovery 73, 79
    Popper's logic of scientific
        discovery 71–72
dissent 28
dream jobs 15–16
drives 33–34
dualism 161–62
duty 113–15
    see also categorical imperative

economics 1, 195
Efficient Market Hypothesis (EMH)
    64–65, 68
emergent strategy 55–56
Emerson, Ralph Waldo 172
emotional engagement see engagement
emotions 135–36
empathy 51–53
employment tribunals 117
empowerment 17–18, 187, 188–89, 194
    authority and 11, 101–22
    empowered organization 195–201
encounter 12, 143, 144–45, 151–63
    changing organizational
        practices 159–61
    implications for leadership 156–58
    presence 155, 156, 161–62
endorsement states 19
engagement 12, 17–18, 143–51, 163
    3E model 97
    Buber 12, 143, 150–51, 152, 156
    buy-in 18, 148–49
    physicality workshop 146–47
    see also encounter
engagement states 19
engagement surveys 17, 143–46
Engels, Friedrich 3
English civil war 110
Enlightenment ideal 175
Enron 12, 29
entrepreneurship 73
Epictetus 11, 123, 130, 131–34
equal liberty, principle of 91
equality 176
    Hobbes and being born equal 110–13
eulogies 15–16
Evans, Paul 183
evidence-based theory 79

example 10–11, 83–99
   Perutz 84–88, 92
   Plutarch 10, 83, 88–90
excellence 22, 34–38
exemplum (moral example) 88–90
existentialism 190, 198–201
expectation 97
experience 135–36, 137
experimentation 74–75, 79–80
expert inquirer mode 133
expertise 128–29
explanation 97

Facebook 4
failure of success 180
fair process dialogue 96–97
fairness 10–11, 83–99
   authority and 109
   Perutz 84–88, 92
   in practice 92–97
   procedural 90–92
fallacy of control 126–27, 132
fallibility, human 67–69, 72
Feldman, Richard 19–20
Fidelity Magellan Fund 62
First World War 199
Fishbanks simulation 47–48
Fitzgerald, F Scott 181
foresight 179
Frankfurt, Harry 77
free will 115, 189–90
freedom 13, 187–202
   empowered organization 195–201
   existentialism 190, 198–201
   Socrates 13, 192–93
   spiritedness 13, 192–95
   Strawson 189–91
French engineering company 5–6
friendship 26
funeral eulogies 15–16

General Electric (GE) 87, 177, 182–83,
   194–95
generosity 26
Germany 113
Ghoshal, Sumantra 38
gift, authority as a 11, 106–09, 110, 121
Glassdoor 33
goal 54
God 199
good intentions, paradox of 75–78
good life 8, 15–23
Google 4
Gore materials company 95–96

government blunders 75–76
groupthink 27–28

Hahn, Kurt 37
Haidt, Jonathan 123, 130, 134, 135–36,
   137, 140
Hamel, Gary 76–77, 106
Hampden-Turner, Charles 181
Haybron, Daniel 19
HCL Technologies 96
Henrich, Joseph 145
heresy 63
heroes 89–90
hierarchy of needs 16
Higher Men 31, 34–36
Hobbes, Thomas 11, 101, 103, 109,
   110–13
honour, protecting 13, 192–95
hospitals 107
human fallibility 67–69, 72
humanity
   categorical imperative 114, 116, 120
   dehumanized workplace 1–8
   strategy and inhumanity 43–45
Hume, David 11, 123, 130, 134,
   138–39, 140
humility 56
hurry sickness 7, 36

I-It interaction 12, 150–51
I-Thou interaction 12, 150, 152–53
Icarus phenomenon 180
ignorance, veil of 10, 91–92
incommensurability 175
incompleteness 155
indecision 179
India 199
Indra's Net 50
inductive logic, discarding 71
industrial workers 2–3
inhumanity, strategy and 43–45
intuition 134
investment bank's values statement
   166–67, 170
investment managers 60–70

Janis, Irving 27
justice 91–92
   and authority 109, 112, 121
   see also fairness

Kant, Immanuel 59, 122, 198–99
   authority 11, 101, 103, 109, 113–17
   categorical imperative 114–18, 171, 198

Kendrew, John 84
key performance indicators (KPIs) 87
Khrushchev, Nikita 52
Kim, W Chan 96–97
kindness 53
King, Anthony 75–76
Kingdom of Ends 114, 116, 120, 191
KKS 160–61
Kotsantonis, Sakis 160–61
Kwan, Savio 194–95

Laboratory of Molecular Biology
    (LMB) 84–88, 92
lattice organization 95–96
learning 147, 181
    encounter and 154–55
learning loop 55–56
Lee, Lance 37–38
libertarians 189
liberty 176
    negative 170
    principle of equal liberty 91
lifestyle change 138–39
lightness of touch 86
London Business School 169
L'Oréal 176–78
Lynch, Peter 62–64, 65–66, 70

Machiavelli, Niccolo 90
Malbec wine 50–51, 59
management psychology see psychology
Mandela, Nelson 192, 193
mantra 45
Marcus Aurelius 131
market discontinuities 68
market inefficiency 64–65
Marx, Karl 2–4, 5
Maslow, Abraham 16
Mauborgne, Renée 96–97
maximin rule 91
MBA students 6
meaningful communication 136–41
meditation 49, 53, 55
meetings
    breakfast meetings 104
    reframing 160, 161
middle way 26–27
    moral dilemmas and 178–79
Milstein, César 85
mind–body separation 161–62
mindfulness 55
mistaken resistance 127–28
mitigating circumstances, absence of 190–91
monarchs 111, 112

moral authority, collapse of 32–33
    see also authority
moral complexity 173–75
    see also pluralism
moral dilemmas see dilemmas
moral sense theory 138
Morgan, Gareth 92
Morning Star 94–95

Nagai, Kiyoshi 85
Nandkishore, Nandu 119–20
Nayar, Vineet 96
Nazism 31, 199
needs, hierarchy of 16
negative liberty 170
neglected polarity 183
Nestlé Philippines 119–20
Nietzsche, Friedrich 9, 22, 30–39, 41
    Nietzschean workplace 35–38
nihilism 33
Nissan 96–97
norms 171
Nozick, Robert 20
Nussbaum, Martha 20

objective observation 150
objective pluralism 175–76
omnipotent leaders 128–30
open-mindedness 78–79
organizational behaviour 90–92
'organize one way, but manage the other'
    principle 183

paradox of good intentions 75–78
paramedics 107
passion
    commitment to act 138–39
    Nietzsche 9, 22, 34–38
path 54–56
pendulum tactic 179
perceptions, survey data and 19–20
person, not role 155
personal responsibility 34
personality 173
Perutz, Max 84–88, 92, 106
pessimism 63
physicality engagement workshop 146–47
Picketty, Thomas 4
plans 54
Plato 192, 193
pleasure machine 20
pluralism 12–13, 169, 173–84
    objective 175–76
    in practice 176–78

Plutarch 10, 83, 88–90
polarization 179
Popper, Karl 10, 60, 68, 69, 70–75, 178
    logic of scientific discovery 71–72
    Popperian theory of corporate
        strategy 72–75
Porter, Michael 45
power 110–13
    see also empowerment
predetermined choices 189
presence 155, 156, 161–62
prison 191–92
    psychic prisons 92
procedural fairness 90–92
psychic prisons 92
psychology 1, 195
    and the good life 8, 15–23

Quantum Fund 68

RAG (Red-Amber-Green) status 148–49
rational activity 115
rationality 72, 78–80
    critical rationalism 71–72, 72–73
    see also critical thinking
Rawls, John 10, 83, 91–93
Raz, Joseph 175
reacting 36
reason (rational thinking) 70, 128–29,
        192–93
    Aristotle 9, 22, 26–30
    commitment to act 138–39
reconciliation 181–83
reflexivity, principle of 69
reframing meetings 160, 161
regrets 197–98, 200
Reitz, Megan 152
relation 150, 152–53, 155
reporting to the customer 96
representative authority 103–04, 111
resistance 126
    mistaken 127–28
Rogue Trader 28
Rousseau, Jean-Jacques 171
Ryle, Gilbert 67

S4 Capital 37
Sadler, Robert 196
Sartre, Jean-Paul 190, 199–200
scientific discovery 71–72
scientific method 67, 72–73, 79
Second World War 52, 199
seeming 152, 155
self-actualization 16–18

self-awareness 33
self-empowerment exercise 196–98
self-interest 115
selfishness 36
Seligman, Martin 21
Seneca 131
Senge, Peter 48
sense giving 139
sense making 136–37, 139–40
sensing 162
sentimentalism 138
set point theory 19
settling 162
sharing 155, 159, 160
shifting 162
siege mentality 49–50
signalling 171
Skilling, Jeff 29
slavery 9, 27–28
Smith, Adam 115
social contract 110–13, 171
socialist regimes 4
Socrates 13, 192–93
somatic knowing 161–62
Soros, George 67–70
Sorrell, Sir Martin 36–37
sovereign ruler 111
speed 62–63
spending rights 107–08, 118
spiritedness 13, 192–95
stoic philosophy 11, 131–34, 140
strategy 9–10, 41–57
    the Buddha 9–10, 48–53, 54–55, 56
    connectedness in action 50–53
    creativity and critical thinking 10, 59–81
    deliberate and emergent 55–56
    and inhumanity 43–45
    Popperian theory 72–75
    value capture and value creation 45–48,
        50, 54, 59
strategy consultants 6, 42–43
Strawson, Peter 189–91
struggle 34–35
suffering 49–50
suggestion schemes 103–04
survey data, problems with 19–20
sustainable competitive advantage 44–48, 51
Sutherland, Rory 77
sweeteners 194–95
Szent-Györgyi, Albert 73

Taylor, Frederick Winslow 4, 92
'tell' approach to communication 11, 123,
        124–30, 132, 151

Thompson, Tommy 52
time
    to develop meaning 136–37
    hurry sickness 7, 36
Titanic Syndrome 48
Town Hall meeting 124–25
traders 28–29
tragedy of the commons 47
training 104
transmit-receive construct 127
tyranny of the tangible 126–27

understanding 134–36
    as a social process 135–36
universalizability 114, 116, 119
upwards delegation 103, 117–18, 121

value capture 45–48, 50, 54, 59
value creation 45–48, 50, 54, 59
values 12–13, 32, 165–85
    Berlin 12, 170, 174–76
    corporate value statements 166–73

dilemmas 168–69, 173–83, 183–84
drives and 33–34
pluralism 12–13, 169, 173–84
reconciliation 181–83
Vasari, Giorgio 90
veil of ignorance 10, 91–92
virtues 12, 26, 173

war of all against all 110–11
Ware, Bonnie 197–98
Watson, Thomas J 65
Welch, Jack 177, 182–83
Will, George 173
Williamson, Oliver 45–46
WL Gore 95–96
'Work-out' 177
World War One 199
World War Two 52, 199
worthwhile pursuits 21
WPP 36–37

Zeno of Citium 131